I Hear Music

I Hear Music

A Physicist Muses on the Quirky Interconnections of Life

Bernard W. Joseph

Over the Transom Publishing Company
Fairhope, Alabama
2001

Over the Transom Publishing Company
323 De La Mare Avenue
Fairhope, AL 36532
email: info@overthetransombooks.com

I Hear Music: A Physicist Muses on the Quirky Interconnections of Life

Library of Congress Control Number: 2001090892
ISBN 0-9643727-7-0

Manufactured in the United States of America

Typeset in Baskerville and Bellevue
Book design by Suzanne S. Barnhill, Words into Type

First Edition 2001

10 9 8 7 6 5 4 3 2 1

Dedication

This book is dedicated to my wife,
who has helped me to sail
through weather thick
and water thin,
figuratively & literally.

Foreword

I started as a child. Dad saw me as an aerial acrobat and started my training early. He built a miniature flying apparatus in the backyard, probably about the time I hit two. I had a photograph of me dressed in some kind of teeny acrobat's tights as I hung from a cane supported by obviously proud Mom and Dad. It got lost during several moves. I vaguely remember swinging in the yard, the smell of tanbark and animals, and cowboys in Wild West shows. According to tales told by my proud Dad, a severe case of measles on the day of my début with the American Legion Circus shot me down in midair, as it were.

My mother thought that I could become a child star of stage and screen. In the late 1920s and early 1930s, many mothers must have thought that. At every song-and-dance school, audition, and cast call to which Mom schlepped me, kids my age filled the hall. Shirley Temple I wasn't, but after a couple of years I became a regular in local productions and radio shows. Too young to know the financial arrangements of entertainment venues in those Depression years, I knew that people threw money on the stage or floor if I was good. Dad usually brought a one-pound coffee sack into which he'd stuff the coins. I kind of think that my income provided the clothes for my sister Barbara and me. About 1934, the people of Detroit voted "Little Billy Joseph" the Star of Tomorrow, presenting me with a nice wrist watch that I remember fell off my wrist. I told the Emcee to try it on my neck. It damned near fit.

Honors do not a career make. By the time I was six or so, song-and-dance faded away. Perhaps my mother saw, after I had started to take that watch apart, that I would make a better mechanic. No one can know what would have been better, but I know that about the time I was ten or eleven I was deep in clocks and radios, taking them apart to see what made them tick and squawk. Even though my Catholic mother would not let me go to Cass Technical High School, I knew that the songs had ended, and that I was bound for science. I enjoyed life as a physicist, having received some honors, a string of citations, and the pure joy of discovery. I made good friends, all of whom respected my scientific abilities, and none of whom respected my singing.

There seems to be a big movement in America today for people to find themselves, to determine what their life is about, to see how they fit into the great plan. I had never felt any need to define myself; I have no need now. But, sometime after I retired, in looking for the words to a song I fondly and frequently mumbled through, I came across two quotes, the first from Sir Winston Churchill, the second from Florence Foster Jenkins:

"I have tunes in my head for every war I've been to, and indeed for every critical or exciting phase of my life."

"Some have said I can't sing. But no one will say that I didn't."

If I were asked to describe the essential me, those excellent words succinctly describe me as I wish I could have myself. Jenkins's are just the thing for my tombstone. After high school, I never performed in public, save as an anonymous tenor in the church choir, or perhaps singing bawdy rugby songs in a pub. But for any time, place, or occasion, I knew a song that described it well, and frequently sang at least a few words. And if I didn't know the complete song, I knew enough of the first words and could ad-lib to do the job. On waking, I might hear "Happy days are here again," on parting with a dear friend, Vera Ellen's "We'll meet again," and because I was thinking of a trip out west, Johnny Mercer's "Atchison, Topeka, and the Santa Fe." I realized that I have gone through life, as Jane Froman frequently sang, "With a song in my heart." The fact that it was frequently on my lips probably bothered a lot of folks, but hey, "I love life, and I've got to live." I did not have to apologize to anyone, I sang.

I'd puttered around writing about how some song perfectly fit the situation in which I found myself. In many cases funny words had popped into mind as I sang. It was not long before I had many snippets on the computer. Over the years, I had occasionally written requests to Leon Cole, host of the CBC-Stereo classical music request program "R.S.V.P." Outside of the radio realm, I'd sent him a couple of drafts of my musical musings, and exchanged email. On his retirement, Leon, aided by his wife Jacqui, wrote a small book based on the requests he'd received. He sent me a copy inscribed, "Joseph, get going on that book. If I can write one, so can you."

So to Leon, who gave me the kick-start, to Thalia Siein yng Nghair, who inspired me to tell stories and encouraged me to write, and to critical daughter Catherine who lovingly corrected and laughed at my stories, I extend thanks. I know these three will read the book.

One

"Hail! Hail! the gang's all here"

Gilbert and Sullivan, 1879

The speed of the human thought process has constantly amazed me. As an unfathomable source of wonder and awe, little compares to it. Those of us who have had a near-death experience speak of the flash before blackout wherein your whole life passes before your eyes. People who survive severe accidents frequently express similar ideas: the event sequence appears in such slow motion that it seems that time has slowed down. But you don't have to come close to death to have such a lightning flash of thought; it happens in even the most mundane situations.

Very frequently I have come to full wakefulness in that short period between the subtle click of the switch on the clock radio and the sound of the music. At times, auditory and visual fireworks accompany that realization of wakefulness. When that happens, the thought flash starts with, "I don't really remember having heard the switch click, but I know it did." Successive thought elements continue with the idea that I'm going to be fully awake in a split-second and then I'll hear the radio playing.

What never ceases to amaze me is that the whole process occurs in a flash, and I know everything that the sequence encompasses. Then the mind seems to run through it again, but this time at a near-normal pace. I find that it takes a minute or two to run that previously instantaneous thought at normal speed. It's as if there's a CLICK, and it's over. In the slow replay, it almost seems as if something gets lost.

The pre-music click this morning started a series of events like that. That particularly amazed me because the Sony radio uses a silent, solid-state switch. But there was a mental CLICK. Instead of fireworks, I saw a flash of a vaguely familiar, musical theater scene. Although I heard neither words nor music, I knew that Gilbert and Sullivan had written them. As I became fully awake, I heard myself singing along with the orchestra that was playing the *Pirates of Penzance* overture. Without my consciously thinking, words to that G&S ditty from Act II came forth. But I didn't sing Gilbert's original "Come, friends, who plough the sea"; nor did I sing the more familiar American chant. Instead, I sang a new set of words.

The words instantaneously popped into mind, in the same manner as WQRS popped up when the clock turned on the radio. From late grammar school days I remember that sort of thing happening, even while wide awake. Some phrases hit my eardrums and then other words stream. The sounds stimulate some portion of the brain, that, like a holographic optical processor, presents a complete picture in an instant. But very frequently, the pictures tend to lean away from the pure.

I remember a General Motors colleague saying: "Joseph, you really have a way with words. Every time we have a group or department meeting or something, you're always quick with a comment that hits the point bang on. I don't know if you're sitting back thinking about them, but it always sounds as if you know the answer before the question. Your words always come out as if you composed them beforehand for publication. Yet somehow, and I don't care what the subject is, or where the meeting is, or who the people are, you always comment in a faintly obscene manner."

I wish I could remember who that colleague was. I thought at first that it was Phil Mohan, who, with the true passion of a good physicist, appreciates scatology, if not all forms of irreverence, and who, with his uncanny ability to detect puffery and fakery and to see the beauty of simple solutions, frequently and adroitly wielded a stuffed-shirt pricker. When I mentioned this to Phil, he alleged that he wasn't the person, even if it sounded like him, but that he thought the description suited me.

I know for sure, the person was male. That eliminates my wife, even though she'd certainly agree with Phil. My penchant to answer questions before the last few syllables are enunciated has driven her to near-violence more than once.

Even if it wasn't Phil, the person saw me better than I did at the time, and, in that remark, opened up a new appreciation of myself, a self that enjoyed the human ability of language, in whatever form it might present itself.

It was probably that inner self that awoke singing:

Hail to the Irish Queen!
What the hell do we care,
If she makes her ass bare?
Hail! Hail! The gang's all here.
I guess that she's embarrassed now.

Two

"He's got hot licks"

Henry Busse, Henry Lange, and
Lou Davis, 1934

Back in the early 1950s, Warren Weaver, in his article on the brain as a computer, said that if they were to build an electronic brain, it would take all Niagara Falls to power it, and all Niagara Falls to cool it. Of course, they didn't have integrated circuits then, and Weaver was speaking of vacuum tubes, such as the U.S. government still uses, and imports from Poland for its IRS computers, but he sketched a great picture: The brain has computing power.

More recently, Paul Churchland gave the human brain capacity as a network of approximately 100 billion neurons and 100 trillion connections. Sounds pretty large to me. Hell! I started in computing when we did it with punched cards, a sorter, and an IBM tabulator. When we got the first IBM Model 650, a real computer with tubes and about 8kB of memory, I thought that we could do everything. But with the brain, we are talking BIG.

Yet, even if one conjectures a huge number of parallel processors, I doubt that the fundamentally serial operation of the individual processors can give such high speed with absolute recognition in a twinkling, based on sparse data. Man! when you see it, you see it now.

This rapidity of memory recovery, under the right circumstances, and the rapidity of object recognition, again, under the right circumstances, constitute two powerful arguments for holographic memory, and an analytical method akin to optical, Fourier-transform data processing. Still, for every one of those brilliant flashes, long moments of utter dullness compensate, like Windows 95 when it gives you one of those Processor Busy messages that ultimately cause you to press CTRL-ALT-DEL.

Sometimes, those blanks, especially when they last a long time, are more in the nature of clear pictures of deep-seated misapprehensions. For example, the song quoted in the heading has been part of my life for a long time. Back in my snapping-whipper days, a favorite uncle liked Henry Busse and used to play his records frequently. I probably heard the song several dozen times. Yet it was only in my dotage that I discovered that the title is "He's Got Hot Lips." "Hot Licks" always sounded good to me. After all, you'd expect a trumpeter to have hot lips, but hot licks made Busse great; hot licks always go through my mind when I think of guys with great chops; and, besides, I had already had sketches of this chapter in my journal before I made the discovery.

At other times, even though the slowness may last for only a short time, the brain pace may decrease to almost full stop. I found myself this morning trying to put on a pair of light, white, sailing shorts I had just retrieved from the drawer. Even though I had worn and loved those shorts for years, this morning they puzzled me. "Son-of-a-gun," I thought, "all the times I've worn these and never noticed they had a button on the inside." For some reason the zipper also presented a puzzle. The pull tab had somehow gotten stuck under the cloth.

"Brother," I mumbled, "one of my jeans is just like this. You'd think the designers would know how to make a zipper placket. They should make the bottom radius smaller; then the tab couldn't drop in the hole." As I struggled, and thought that perhaps I would have to get a screwdriver or pliers to prise the tab out, a dim light struggled to make itself seen.

"Jesus! that's really funny. The seams are all raveled. Son-of-a-bitch! Goddamn! I musta run them through the washing machine twice. Shit! my favorite shorts ruined. No, can't be, none of the other stuff got screwed up."

The light became brighter as I struggled with the recalcitrant zipper, until my stupidity shone in its brilliance: I had the shorts on inside out.

We all have puzzling days like that. Sometimes, those puzzles go on for months.

Rich Hibbner had seen my amateur radio license plates many times when I parked in the lot at GM's Milford Proving Ground. Rich knew that the State of Michigan had vanity plates. He knew that most people who have vanity plates put letters and numbers on them that have some meaning. You know, something readable like MY CAR or CHEVY2, or something that might be initials, like Jon McLeod's JRM. But to Rich, K8LIX was a puzzle.

Many a day he would pause as he passed my car in the lot, looking and wondering what K8LIX meant on Joseph's vanity plate. Rich didn't know that the State of Michigan also had special call sign plates for amateur radio operators. One day he stopped me out in the dyno area of the lab and told me of his problem: "I know that the plates on your car mean something, but I've been trying to figure it out and I'm stumped. It almost looks like there's a Kate something, but I sure don't know what it means. It's probably something dirty, right?"

"It sure is. And man, did I have to work to trick the State into putting dirty words on a plate. Those suckers up in Lansing must have a computer with every variety of every dirty word in every language in it. I got kicked out a lotta times before I came up with this."

"Then what the hell does it mean? It doesn't look too dirty."

"Well Rich, figure it out. My girlfriend's name is Katrina and her tongue..." I didn't have to continue. With a grin of cognition, Rich walked away, happy that his opinion of Bill Joseph was correct.

Rich worked in Test Ops for several more years, until he married a German girl and moved there to work at the Opel lab at Russelheim. During the remainder of his Milford tenure, we passed many times in the hall and bumped into each other in the john. On most of those passings and pissings, Rich smiled knowingly at me. Once in a while he'd ask how Kate was. I wonder if the light ever dawned.

Three

"I've gotta crow"

Carolyn Leigh and Moose Charlap, 1954

As far as I know, there aren't too many men who have taken up the side of women in battling their problem of insufficient public *pissoirs.* I am on their side. Whenever opportunity presents itself—which isn't too often—I make a plea for relief and urge women to fight for their right.

When Robin Abcarian, then writing for the *Detroit Free Press,* brought up the subject, I wrote to her stating my support, and outlining an aid to future improvements. The design of every *pissoir* should recognize the simple anatomical fact that a woman can pee farther than a man, and that's with no hands. If you doubt that, consider a mare and a stallion. The mare will squirt a stream quite a distance to her rear; the stallion pees all over his feet. Every architect takes Bathroom 101 in college, yet they seem they seem to have forgotten that.

Like architects, clothing designers have forgotten too. With the possible exception of some sportswear, I have never seen any men's pants that don't have a fly in front. But I have never seen any women's wear that has a fly in the rear. Designers, and the retailers who promote those deficient wares, even penalize women further with all-in-one underwear and the likes of Spandex jumpsuits. I just can't imagine having to pee like hell and then having to peel off two tight layers. Even with a drop crotch on the second layer, one must struggle.

Robin answered, expressing amazement and thanks that a man would appreciate the problem, would have given it serious thought, and would support women in trying to obtain more equitable facilities. For that, a bit of pride swells in me and I feel that I can crow.

We exchanged letters on the subject for a while, hammering out our ideas on mechanics, doing a bit of cursory checking to see if anything is being done, and informing each other of customs that we knew about in other times and countries. Ms. Abcarian finally noted that, along with architectural and clothing modifications, it would be necessary to change the very fundamental social habit that women must sit to pee. We agreed that the last change appears to present an insurmountable impediment.

My familiarity with this problem stems from our regular theater attendance. The Hilberry lacks loos; the elegant Fisher barely makes it; the DIA Film Theater hits a new low. In every case, before first curtain, at the intermissions, and frequently at the end of the performance, well-dressed women, the older crammed into their one-piecers, the younger into their Spandex jumpsuits, stand with thighs pressed tightly together, pretending to chat amiably as each bladder becomes more insistent. I wonder how women can continue to just take it. Why, with all this force behind them, don't they stand up for their rights and fight for stand-up *pissoirs*—and the clothes to go along with them? Why don't they raise their fists and give the female Black Panther cry, "All power to the peers?"

While standing in the DIA's elegantly shabby basement hall, waiting for Hildegard to come out of the restroom, watching the line barely getting shorter, and talking to another male waiter, the first lines of a campaign song came to mind:

> I've gotta go.
> I don't feel fine
> Cuz I'm standing in line,
> And the line is too slow.
> I gotta go.

𝄋

Four

"Animal crackers in my soup"

Ted Koehler, Irving Caesar, and
Ray Henderson, 1935

In early October 1991 I saw just a bit of a television item about Ambassador Shirley Temple Black. It showed her, in 1974, presenting her credentials as Ambassador Extraordinary and Plenipotentiary to the President of Ghana. He, in his military uniform replete with those fictitious decorations characteristic of Third-World leaders, surrounded by equally decorated bobs and nabobs, with his haughty glare down his nose, laid his African emperor shtick on Mrs. Black.

In a circumstance such as that, I would have been tempted to say, "Your show doesn't impress me, sir. You're a third-rate head of a third-world country, but I have a job to do. Big Daddy Ford wants me to keep an eye out for what's going on, and I'm gonna do that. See you around." But Mrs. Black, she of most elegant bearing and demeanor, followed the form required. She did great credit to the U.S.A. and American women in the presentation, as well as throughout her tenure.

Although I haven't followed every move of Mrs. Black, partly because she doesn't seem to seek the limelight, I know that she moved to a higher position as ambassador to Czechoslovakia in 1988. When a reporter asked her whether she thought she was qualified for such a position, in view of her background as a song-and-dance person, she said that the people of the country had had many sorrowful days, and they would probably like to sing and dance as they work toward freedom after years of oppression. Touché!

Those little bits I have seen have made my respect for her grow. My impression of most people in show business, and in the movies in particular, is that they don't have much as a person to fall back on when they are not on stage or camera. It is almost as if their only life is that of a script, their only actions those given by a director. But those little bits showed me that Shirley doesn't belong to that class.

Shirley impressed people in the whole world. I remember reading something quite a few years ago about poor outdoor theaters in Africa running her pictures over and over because the people love the little curly-head so much. Her bounce and verve appeal to all, even if they don't understand the words. If more were told about her current actions, I'm sure that the impression of her good work would continue also.

She did much to inspire and educate women on breast cancer, at a time when we didn't talk about it, and TV made a lot of that. But, perhaps because of her statements during the Vietnam war, the communication media don't pay much attention to her now. That's too bad. Today, when punk, grunge, designer stubble, ill-fitting clothes, backward hats, and the generally uncouth, boorish, unschooled, and unwashed behavior that goes with them have taken over most every person below the age of forty, Mrs. Black, she of the "unconscious sense of dignity," as her school teacher said of her, could be as much a role model for mature life now as she is for today's junior song-and-dancers, and their teachers, who still love the "Curly Top" of 1935.

I would bet that if one walked into the Borgo Sisters' School of Dance in Royal Oak or the Dubuque Drama Workshop, one would see a five-year-old learning to sing "Animal Crackers," and the kid would be trying to use the same motions and facial expressions that Shirley Temple used. Most likely the kid would be a little girl, but even little boys have learned the words. As one of my music-teacher friends told me, they teach the songs in kindergarten or the first grade in many public schools. Maybe they even use Shirley Temple songs in preschools.

It's with a twinge of mixed emotions that I remember what went through my mind some time ago. About twenty years ago we had dinner at the home of our friends Jovan and Bogdanka Bjelobrk. Their five-year-old daughter Dragana popped, bopped, and jumped around the house. I couldn't quite hear what she was singing because she never dropped below sonic speed.

"She's going to dance school," Bo said. "Dragana, come over here and show Mr. Joseph what you've learned. He used to sing on the radio when he was your age. He might even know some of the songs."

Indeed I did, especially "Animal Crackers." I sang silently along with her:

> Animal crappers in my soup;
> I really hate it when they poop.
> Gosh! Oh gee! it sure ain't fun,
> Watching them wallowing in their dung.

Ambassador Black, I apologize.

Five

"You do something to me"

Cole Porter, 1952

In the final scene of the 19 August 1991 episode of *Northern Exposure,* Maggie O'Connell puts a cassette into the player and dreamily dances out of the room to the vocal refrain of "You do something to me / something that really mystifies me." That scene will stick in my memory for a long time.

First, because the first few sounds of the vocalist's voice struck a favorite music chord: a beautiful female voice backed up by a barroom piano, like Michelle Pfeiffer's in *The Fabulous Baker Brothers,* if I may use an Ed Chigliak movie simile. I have a number of things like that in my music collection, as well as records of some great male vocalists such as Mel Torme and Michael Feinstein. That laid-back feeling of such artists, even when they're scatting, along with the pure enjoyment of the movement of fingers and vocal cords, gets down deep inside me.

Second, because the actor so beautifully caught the tenderness of the momentous realization that one's mystifying feelings for another might be love. In just the way she moved out of the room with a gentle sway and a faint look back to the player, she conveyed the appropriate *je ne sais quoi* that made it seem so right and beautiful.

And third, because I, after having watched almost all the episodes of the series, just then realized how subtly and wonderfully some responsible person had consistently woven great theme music into the continuing drama.

Consider the difference in feeling if the producer had chosen "This can't be love, because I feel so well." Constant viewers know that the cat-and-dog antagonism between O'Connell and Fleischman is slowly developing into love. The use of such an obvious musical statement would have telegraphed the outcome. Alternatively, the producer could also have used a somewhat more subtle piece, such as "You made me love you," or "I don't know why I love you like I do." But in my estimation, even one of the latter seems more akin to a musical baseball bat than to a musical feather. The use of the "You do something" theme emphasizes the feeling that O'Connell, sensing the kindling of a dim flame, still doesn't quite know what is happening; the mystery deepens, and the viewer stays hooked for the finale.

This realization of the fine line the producer trod to deliver an extremely powerful message so adroitly and economically caused me to wonder about the mental processes that go into selection. No doubt a computer formalism exists that permits one to do this by simply following certain rules. But I would prefer to believe that the producer, or producer's delegate, came up with the choice by intuition, that powerful ability to add two and two and come up with five, six, or, for exceptional intuiters, ten. I admire that ability.

To many people, the three reasons given suffice and make sense because they feel something akin. In my case, a fourth reason came to mind as I realized that, for the first time, I had heard those words without being reminded of the version that I had mentally sung for many years. As the recipient at a *bris* might sing to the *mohel:*

> You'll do something to me,
> Something that really mystifies me.
> Tell me why should it be,
> You have big shears to circumcise me?

Even though I'd like it to be a little longer, I think I'll cut this essay off with that.

𝄋

Notes

bris: circumcision ceremony

mohel: a person who performs circumcisions

Six

"I'd like to teach the world to sing"

Billy Davis, Bill Backer, Roger Cook, and
Roger Greenaway, 1971–1972

The economic and business press frequently carry articles postulating the existence of predictable cycles in economics and business. A big deal right after the stock market's Black Monday in 1987 was the Elliott Wave Theory. The theory predicted that things were going to get worse.

To a large extent I have not paid much attention to this subject, primarily because I think that chaos governs both arenas. The country's or world's economy, and a nation's or company's business, may go up and down, but that does not signify cycles to me. As for Elliott, he missed out on one of the biggest booms in our country's history.

Perhaps my long association with radio, not as the performer of my youth, but as a licensed commercial operator, as a physicist, and as an amateur radio operator, has nuked my brain, but that association has also convinced me that cycles imply periodicity. If you can't write down the Fourier decomposition of the string of events in a fairly simple manner, and with just a few terms, then you're only talking about ups and downs.

Apparently, the market forecasters have never taken the obvious math courses. And there are plenty of forecasters around. Advertisements for their get-rich-quick books and courses abound in the financial papers. Many of the ads have a graph of a market or stock performance with arrows pointing to peaks and valleys, and showing how, had you bought the book last year, you could have become rich. Of course, all these performance charts show quite precisely what happened in the past. I'm looking for the one that shows me what to do in the future.

I'm pretty sure that that won't happen, certainly not in my lifetime, if ever. As Jeremy Siegel, professor of finance at the Wharton School of Finance, said in *Investor's Business Daily,* 10 December 1998, "You could have the most powerful computer in the world and you still would not be able to build a mathematical model that can beat the market over the long haul. The market is not totally random, but it is random enough so that no one can crack it."

We hear about these almost-periodic cycles in other things as well. As a sailor, I've heard of the seventh-wave theory, or maybe it was the fifth-wave theory. No matter. The theory holds that every seventh (fifth) wave is a big one. I could almost believe it myself, having tried to time my sailing accelerations to catch that seventh (fifth) wave for a wild surf. It sure seems as if it works.

But I figured out why some people say it's the seventh wave whereas others assert that it's the fifth, or maybe the third. The fact is, it's either all of the above or none of the above. Real waves are not all uniform. If you stand watching them long enough, you seem to see a pattern. After you have observed enough waves, you might hypothesize a pattern. It's simple enough to test; I propose the Armani-Gucci test protocol.

Put on your Armani suit, the silk one with trousers that overhang your heel. Put on your best Gucci loafers, the snakeskin ones preferably. Walk down to the beach on a breezy day and establish the pattern to your satisfaction. After the big wave, walk down to the edge of the little wave line, and stand there with your back to the ocean. Count the waves, and move deftly higher up the beach just before the big one hits. I bet you get soaked more often than you stay dry. Although God was supposed to have brought Order out of Chaos, He left enough chaos around to make beach walks interesting.

Meteorologists try to find similar patterns in order to better predict weather. On the Great Lakes, my sailing logs indicate that they are right about half the time. In one of the sailing magazines, I read a letter that gave the same success rate for the eastern seaboard of the United States. It's not just a problem of insufficient data on past behavior; atmospheric waves behave pretty much as God let oceanic waves do.

Sound waves exhibit similar behavior. As Margaret Cheney showed in her *American Scientist* article on remote sensing, sound waves from a seismograph, as used in oil exploration, can easily and precisely determine the shape of a single structure. But with the presence of a second structure, reverberations between the two prevent anything more than an approximation to the real solution.

In his book *Chance and Chaos,* David Ruelle put it, "...many physical systems exhibit sensitive dependence on initial condition for arbitrary initial condition. This is somewhat counterintuitive, and it has taken some time for mathematicians and physicists to understand well how things happen." Never mind about complex problems with many variables, such as meteorology, seismology, or the stock market, some extremely simple problems can't be fully solved, even by great computers and great minds.

For example, if you have a system that has two objects in it, say a sun and a planet, or an electron and proton, it's straightforward physics to calculate the motion of the system. You can calculate position, velocity, momentum, energy, etc., for each object and the system rather easily. We do have the Heisenberg uncertainty principle in operation when we get to the atomic level; otherwise, with ordinary objects in ordinary space you know exactly where the two objects are at any instant. But if you introduce a third object into the system, the analysis falls apart completely. It is simply impossible to solve the classical three-body problem. Peculiar, eh?

> I'd like to get my balls to swing
> In perfect harmony.
> I'd walk downtown without my pants
> For every one to see.

The one swings left, the other right,
In pure harmonic motion.
The third one swings the way it wants,
And that's a mystery.

Seven

"Song sung blue"

Neil Diamond, 1972

Jessica Ross's mondegreen Web site is a kick. Her compilation of the way that people mishear music lyrics makes me laugh every time I read it. It's the old difference between stimulus and perception at work. In contrast to the popular dictum, "What you see is what you get," what you hear is not always what you think you heard. Reichert Virgil said he heard Diamond's words as "Selsun Blue."

Having gone to a Catholic school, I know that a lot of children, for example, when reciting the Hail Mary, say "Blessed is the Fruit of the Loom, Jesus." I can relate to that: how many second-graders know about wombs? If you don't know the actual words, words that come close suffice. That applies to adults as well.

My friend Phil Mohan fondly relates how he misapprehended Gilbert and Sullivan's "Poor Wandering One" when he was in high school. Phil was working the technical part when his school produced *Pirates of Penzance*. In their production, the pirates sat around a table drinking during the song. Taking all these visual cues, Phil thought that the song was "Pour one, drink one." He went many years before he heard the real words.

In contrast to Phil's mondegreen in high school, one of my own ended in my freshman year at St. Anthony high school. I don't know where it started, but I would guess the fourth or fifth grade when kids start singing folk songs in school. It also must have happened when I learned the song without sheet music or, at least, printed words. In the chorus of "There is a Tavern in the Town," I'd sing: "I do, I do, I do, I do, yes, I do. It was not until a choral music class in the ninth grade that I read: "Adieu, adieu," etc., and realized my mistake.

Given the circumstances of these three examples, it's easy to understand the mondegreens. But shouldn't adults have heard and known the simple words song, sung, and blue? Unlike Frankie Valli's slurvanism in Crewe's song "My Eyes Adored You," which comes out sounding like "I buys ya Georgia," Diamond's excellent diction lets the words come through clearly. So why did Reichert Virgil tell Jessica that he heard "Selsun Blue"?

I'm willing to give Reichert credit for having written it as he heard it. But I suspect that many who have other words to songs have thought about those words for quite a while before they got them to fit. I figure that their reactions are miles away from Reichert's possibly instantaneous mondegreen, and my own lightning compositions.

Did a dandruff problem stimulate him to hear those words? I kind of think it may have in my own case. In a vain attempt to get my hair to the point where women want to run their hands through it, I've used a lot of

Selsun Blue. The FDA approved it, so somebody thinks that it works as intended. But I'm not sure that it does much more than a simple shampoo job would. Except for my wife, and a nymphomaniacal acquaintance of years ago, women keep their hands out of my hair.

Much to my amazement, the communication media, along with the drug companies, have not made much of the recently discovered medical fact that a yeast infection causes the persistent form of dandruff. Oh, one or two ads have appeared in the Sunday supplements stating that you can see your doctor for a prescription for a new shampoo, but I would have expected an advertising deluge, similar to that for sinus remedies. Surely, falling scalp flakes induce as deep a concern for one's social health as does a stuffed or drippy nose.

I've solved the problem for myself. I figure that if GyneLotrimin® can kill one kind of yeast it might be able to kill another. I buy brand X seven-day yeast treatment at my local Perry drug store. I put a good squirt in the palm of my hand, pour in a bit of shampoo, mix it up to form a nice goo, and lather my hair. I usually lather up and let the stuff work while I shave. The yeast medication instructions say not to get it in the eyes, so I have to wipe my forehead a couple of times during the process. But that minor inconvenience aside, I'm very happy with the results. When used thrice weekly, it works a lot better than any dandruff shampoo, and it seems to sooth the scalp, unlike patent remedies that make it tingle.

I never told Dr. Sadoff, my dermatologist, about my home-brew dandruff shampoo. I'm sure she'd pull down the *Physician's Desk Reference,* or get one of those fine-print information sheets, to give me some line about what the indications and contraindications are for the drug used in the yeast medication. She'd tell me that there's no information on reactions with the scalp, etc. She'd tell me all about the dangers of self-medication. She probably wouldn't listen to my argument that my upper region is probably not as sensitive as her nether region.

Selsun Blue,
You're killing all my dandruff.

Selsun Blue,
You're making my old scalp rough.

Eight

"Rudolph, the red-nosed reindeer"

Johnny Marks, 1949

When we moved to the Glenbrook Meadows condominium in late November 1993, it took us a while to find a satisfactory furniture arrangement for the living room. We were at a loss for where to put the Christmas tree until one of us realized that we could put it on the deck that ran between the dining room and living room. It turned out to be a splendid arrangement. I had to improvise a wooden base because the tree refused to stay up in the stand we had used indoors for years.

With a firm base, and a couple of nylon monofilament fishing lines tied to strategic points on the deck, it now stood upright before our living room window. That is, it stood until the wind piped up. It seems that the line of two condominium blocks curving from southeast to northwest funnels every wind right down the common area.

Although I have not analyzed it carefully, I think that the Bernoulli effect increases the wind velocity so that it reaches a maximum right at our deck. After finding that neither a reasonable number of strings nor increased triangulation of the base would hold the tree upright against the December winds, we moved it to a protected corner where we could see it from the dining room table. With some silver garlands, a few weatherproof baubles, and miniature lights that finally worked after I found the defective one at the end of the last of six strings, it made Christmas real in the new home.

The grandkids weren't too sure that we knew about Christmas. To them, a tree on the deck was a tree on the deck, but it wasn't a real Christmas tree. Nate was too young to talk about it, but Tom and Pete had quite a few questions and statements about the propriety of having the tree outside.

In 1994 we put a four-foot spruce in the corner next to the stereo cabinet in the living room. Except for the heat from the lights disturbing the furnace thermostat, I thought it was a pretty good arrangement. The grandkids thought it was a real Christmas, especially the youngest, who, like his brothers before him, thought that the little fuzzy walking Rudolph toy was the neatest thing he had ever seen. He, without instruction, followed the tradition of lying on the kitchen floor and squealing as Rudolph walked around, nose alight, head nodding, and playing Christmas carols through his belly speaker until the batteries wore out. He's too young to understand Grandpa's Christmas song, even if Grandma had let Grandpa sing it.

Red Rolf, the rude-nosed reindeer,
Had a very funny nose.
And if you ever saw it,
You would know just where it goes.

Nine

"I'se the b'y that builds the boat"

Traditional Canadian

In years gone by I'd thought about building a boat. It had been a near-lifetime dream. In my Navy days, I spent many an hour looking at the plans published in *Rudder* and in reading Chappelle and other great writers on the subject. While stationed at Glenview Naval Air Station, not too far from Lake Michigan, I spent many evenings with fellow rigger Nelson Molson drinking Harvey's Bristol Cream sherry and talking about that blue-water trip we'd do after our discharge.

We even went so far as to buy an old 12-foot sailboat that we planned to restore and learn on. Boy, were we green. The boat was in such bad shape that we never sailed it. We didn't even repair it, let alone restore it.

Right after my discharge, I followed a friend's lead and applied for a job as a deckhand on a big sailboat moored at the Grosse Pointe Yacht Club. As I remember, it was owned by a big wheel in the automobile industry. Because I dawdled about instead of going down immediately to the Coast Guard office in Detroit to get my seaman's papers, I didn't get the job. No matter.

I forwent the sailing experience and, at the urging of my intended wife, got an honest job with General Motors at the Research Laboratories, got married shortly thereafter, and started to raise a family almost immediately.

In late 1952 or early 1953, I was invited to join the North Star Sail Club by the son of a member who knew of my sailing interests. The club had undergone a loss of membership and was looking for bodies. My excuse that I didn't have a sailboat brought the rejoinder that "A lot of members don't. They're building their own plywood jobs." For whatever reason, I declined the invitation. But in the mid- to late '60s, my friend and North Star member Tom Schreiber bought a Cal 25 and asked me to crew. We spent some great years in the money in most races because of Tom's excellence.

By this time, the builder itch had long vanished. Fiberglass had replaced wood as the material of choice for boats. It was now a lot easier to buy a good boat than to build it, but I never thought of owning one. Well, we did have part ownership in a Grumman canoe with a sailing rig, but that hardly counts.

How the owner urge returned escapes recollection, but in 1979 Hildegard and I took the beginner's and the cruising courses at Annapolis Sailing School, chartered a Seaforth in Lake Erie for two weeks when we returned, and decided we both liked sailing. Late that year we bought a Columbia 8.3, named her *La Yu,* and spent much joyful time over several years sailing Lakes St. Clair, Huron, and Erie.

When 1986 and my retirement rolled around, we decided to take the leap. After selling *La Yu* to Carl

Schulte, who still owns and sails her regularly, we went to Florida, hired a local surveyor who didn't know anything about sailboats, bought a 1964 Alberg 35, and shipped it back to Michigan. I didn't plan on becoming a boat builder; I only planned to fix up the rough edges, test-sail her on the Great Lakes, and then make our way to exotic places and Paradise.

Hildegard and I had taken quite a lot of time deciding on a name. One cannot treat naming as a trivial matter when the vessel is to be your home and transportation to see the world. With music such a strong part of lives, we were pretty sure that the name would have to be on a musical line. You see a lot of *Andante*s, *Adagio*s, *Vivace*s, and such on the water. We tried to think of something not so common. I suggested *Polonaise,* not only musical, but a statement of our heritage. In a stroke of musical, punning, and historical brilliance, Hildegard came up with *ASTIGAFA*.

Perfect! The boat came from the Beatles period; the name is an acronym for "A Splendid Time Is Guaranteed For All"—with an extra *A* thrown in for easy pronunciation. John Lennon sings the words at the end of the song "Being for the Benefit of Mr. Kite" from the Sgt. Pepper album. We certainly expected to have a splendid time on her in Paradise.

Actually, Marshall Crenshaw came up with that name for his first band and their first recording studio in Royal Oak. Since the name was legally registered, we probably should have asked his permission to use it. But Marshall had honed his trade in our basement, his band cracking the plaster, gouging the walls, shaking the putty out of the windows, loosening doorknob screws, and (infrequently) bringing the Berkley police to knock on our door asking the guys to pipe down. We figured he owed us.

The boat arrived at North River Road Marina on the Clinton River. My good friend, ham radio buddy, and sailboat rigger extraordinary, Jon Kaplan (R.I.P., old friend), took a look at her as the semi pulled in and said, "Boy! You sure bought a piece of shit, didn't you."

"Well, I have to fix up a couple of things."

"You're gonna sail this around the world?"

"Maybe not all the way."

"Ya better stick around here for a while."

I had prepared a new plate for the transom to cover up the original *Casta Diva,* and went through the propitiation ceremony attendant to changing the name of a vessel. Though the moon was not visible, I begged her indulgence, and promised to play her aria from Donizetti's *Norma* when I got home. I offered a Christian prayer; I said *shalom* and *mazel tov* several times; I mumbled *chakran* to Allah and *arrigato* to Buddha; I poured wine into the river for Neptune; I passed out cigars and offered the smoke to Aeolus; I made offering to the four corners to ask Manitou's blessing; following Chinese tradition I lit a row of firecrackers to drive away evil spirits. I didn't know how many to use, but a dozen, to represent the zodiac, seemed appropriate. I lined them up on a board under the transom and touched them off in turn with my cigar. The last firecracker just fizzled.

"You're fucked now," said Jon.

I knew that Jon was the best rigger on the river; I didn't know he was a seer. As I backed the boat out of the launch slip to turn it around so we could step the mast, I heard a loud clunk, the wheel spun out of my grip, and the boat circled backward, helpless in mid-river. After the rescue boat, for a pair of 20-dollar bills, towed me back to the slip, I determined that loose set screws had permitted the prop shaft to spin itself out of the coupling. The loud clunk was the prop slamming into the rudder and jamming it against the stop. That was fortunate in a way. Had the prop not been in a rudder aperture, the whole shaft would have come out of the boat, and water would have poured in through the hole. More than one boat has sunk because of that.

Like it or not, I became a boat builder at that instant. With makeshift tools of an unbelievably crude nature, I got the shaft back into the coupler, secure enough for a cautious trip downriver to my home well, hoping all the time that I wouldn't have to use reverse. After going aground on a sandbar and maneuvering gingerly for about ten minutes, all to the delight of shore folk watching, I got afloat and got home.

Hildegard and I spent five years rebuilding the boat. We did some great summer sailing in her, hitting all the Great Lakes save Ontario, which we planned to sail on our way out. But the remaining nine months of each year were spent in blood, sweat, and tears. Between us, we acquired about five new scars, a few dozen stitches, a cracked rib, a couple of torn ligaments, an occasional utter hatred of each other and the boat, and, ultimately, respect for each other and the boat.

We had some good sailing times. *ASTIGAFA* took us to all the Great Lakes, the St. Lawrence and Hudson rivers, through 64 locks, along the Atlantic coast to Chesapeake Bay and back. We accomplished part of the dream with some splendid moments.

We navigated through pea-soup fog and rocks in Lake Superior to find a magnificent anchorage in the Agawa Islands. As we went through Quebec's Chambly canal system, that takes you from the St. Lawrence River to Lake Champlain, we happily thought that we were in France. In Sandy Hook bay, Hildegard harvested enough mussels for two meals and a couple of snacks. She had always wanted to do that. We had a really splendid time in Annapolis when our daughter visited us. We three stuffed ourselves at a raw bar on local clams, oysters, and crabs.

Even some of the bad times had an element of goodness, if only because one realized a sense of accomplishment. Having to dive sans wetsuit in 64-degree water to verify that we had indeed broken the rudder was not pleasant going in nor in staying under. Yet, the exhilaration following the dive, and the pride in being able to fashion a jury rudder and get us safely to Annapolis made up for some of the misery.

However, in spite of five years' cleanup work, the remnants of the fizzled firecracker stayed with us. I'll not repeat the problem litany: a pair of interviews by *Great Lakes Sailor* magazine covered it well. Because of all the work that it took to keep *ASTIGAFA* going, and my own uneasiness, we didn't get to the white sands, palm trees, and blue skies. It's great out there, but it's not Paradise.

I'se the b'y that builds the boat,
And I'se the b'y that sails her.
Been in a berth with many a girl,
But never Elizabeth Taylor.

Ten

"Listen / Do you want to know a secret?"

John Lennon and Paul McCartney, 1963

Lucius Tripp, M.D., Director, Medical Services, General Motors Proving Ground. Just roll that name around your tongue for a bit. Lucius Tripp, Lucius Tripp, Lucius Tripp. Surely it conjures up an image. Perhaps you think of the many great Romans: Lucius Cornelius Alexander Polyhistor, Lucius Caecilius Firmianus Lactantius, or just plain Lucius who later became just plain Nero. Perhaps you think of a more modern example, such as General Lucius Clay, who made his mark during World War II, or General Lucius Clay, Jr., who did the same during the Vietnam action.

In any case, I'd bet that the image was one of a distinguished man, tall, possibly acerbic, probably bearing a mustache, and wearing elegant clothes. That, dear friend, describes Dr. Tripp fairly well. I think that his lab coats came from Brooks Brothers. In addition to his good bearing, or maybe because of it, Lucius had good manners and graciousness. He handled his managerial and medical duties in an excellent manner.

Because I worked with hazardous materials at the Proving Ground, I received an annual medical examination at Medical Services. Actually, GM's official name for the procedure was "medical evaluation." Apparently, as Lucius explained to me, it had to do with insurance, workers' compensation, or other arcane legal matters. Doesn't matter what they called it, it was a full medical examination. I rather enjoyed them. In part, the enjoyment came from the efficient manner in which the Service handled it; in part it came because they had some good-looking nurses and technicians.

An outstanding technician handled tests like EKG, audiology, and pulmonary function. I'm five foot two. When we stood face-to-face, I looked squarely at her eyebrows. I don't know her measurements, but I estimate that had she been five-seven, she would have been a 36-24-34. Need I say that she looked like a Breck girl? Although she cut her blond hair fairly short, the way she curled it gave it the same kind of bounce that the rest of her exhibited. She reminded me a lot of Betty Hutton. In fact, I think her name was Betty.

For people like me who handled toxic gases, such as carbon monoxide and nitrogen oxides, Medical Services emphasized the importance of the pulmonary function test. It was also part of the research that Dr. Tripp was doing.

Betty did her job well and expected clients to do the same. She reiterated the instructions about the importance of the test and had me do a practice run, at the end of which she said, "You can do better than that, I'm sure. You look like you're pretty fit and you don't smoke. Let's get those volumes up near the top of the chart. I'll help you."

"Okay! Just tell me what to do."

"Just do what I tell you."

I put the mouthpiece between my teeth and took the big breath.

"Get your shoulders up! Inhale! Inhale! Inhale! Good! Good! Good! Now exhale hard. Hard, I said hard! Harder! Harder! Deeper! Deeper! Harder! More! More! More! Deeper! Deeper! That's good! Good! Dee—"

The lab door burst open and Tripp stood there saying, "What's going on in here?"

I damned near choked.

"We're just finishing Mr. Joseph's pulmonary test."

"God! Do you know what it sounds like out in the hall? A little quieter next time, okay?" He gently closed the door.

Fortunately, in spite of the abrupt termination, Betty's coaching helped me get up to about the 95th percentile for my age group. We chatted for a bit and laughed about what happened. "I know what it sounded like in here. It was just a pulmonary test. But I would like to have been in hall to hear what Dr. Tripp heard. I can see where he might have some concerns," I said.

"I wonder if he's going to say anything about it to anyone else? It would make a good story, even if it was kinda embarrassing. I should have known better than to get so excited."

I assured her that I wouldn't tell anybody. I think I may have told my wife shortly after it happened. And I think that much later I told the story to Tom Schreiber,

Phil Mohan, and maybe Jovan Bjelobrk, all close and close-mouthed GM associates and friends. If I violated the letter of my assurance, I think I kept the spirit.

The prostate check was a voluntary part of the exam. I volunteered, figuring that there must be a good reason why Tripp suggested it. A lot of guys, feeling a bit funny about that part of the exam, didn't volunteer. I understood their feelings.

For many years we've had ads in magazines, on radio and television, and on billboards telling women to check their breasts and to have regular mammograms. We've come a long way on the road of destigmatizing this subject since Shirley Temple Black first made public her bout with breast cancer. We haven't gone as far as the British, with their forty-foot—or should I say twelve-meter?—billboards of a nubile young woman examining her breasts, but we do show drawings in the newspapers, and color photographs in women's magazines of the process. I gather that the health statistics show it's working. We've made a significant dent in the breast cancer problem.

Men don't talk about their health problems as problems, even though they might joke about them. For as long as I can remember, older guys all joked about how hard it was to pee, and how frequently they had to do it. It's hard to get it going, and it's hard to shut it off. The best we can do is to take urination termination slowly enough that drips end up in our shorts, rather than down the front of our pants.

Until recently, we haven't talked too much about the prostate problem that is at the root of poor peeing. I'm really glad to see that the health gurus have recently come up with a good program to get the message out to men. They have George Foreman saying, "Real guys get it checked." Today, you can get the PSA test done on a blood sample, but the classic digital palpation still gives immediate feedback to the physician.

Dr. Tripp's elegant manner seemed to change somewhat when we got to that part of the exam. "Drop your trousers and underpants, spread your legs, and lean over," he brusquely instructed, with his latex-enveloped right hand raised and a very large tube of K-Y jelly in the left.

Maybe it was the room-temperature K-Y jelly; maybe Tripp normally had cold hands. The sensation of that abrupt cold-digit entry into the warm cavity made one pucker up. But in an instant it was over.

"Here, wipe yourself," he said, handing me couple of paper towels. Man! he must have had stock in K-Y: the two sheets barely sufficed to clean oneself. Of course, since he had already left the room, you could walk over to the towel dispenser with your pants around your ankles, like Lily Tomlin in "Search for Inteligent Life in the Universe." That is, if the jelly didn't start to melt and run down your legs. Then you had to do a quick hop. Over a couple of years I got pretty good at the drill.

As part of my work with lasers, GM sent me to Henry Ford Hospital for yearly ophthalmological exams. When I retired, I decided to stay with HFH for all my medical needs, and became a patient of Dr. Patricia Holsey. Her office on Woodward was close enough so that I could take my bike or walk there, weather permitting. Her method and manner during the prostate exam differed substantially from that of Tripp.

In the first place, she palpated while I lay on my side on the examination table. In the second place, she inserted the finger slowly and gently, all the while giving me relaxation instructions. Thirdly, she didn't own stock in K-Y. Judging by the small amount she used, she may have had to buy it herself. Lastly, she did the cleanup herself.

Closer,
Shove your finger up my rear.
I will promise not to yell,
Oh oh oh oh.
Closer.

Eleven

"Vaya con Dios, my darling"

Larry Russell, Inez James, and
Buddy Pepper, 1953

Hildegard thought that Dr. Holsey was adequate. She felt that the doctor didn't take as much time in explanations as she would have liked. I was very satisfied with Holsey. In fact, I thought she was warm and friendly.

During one of my yearly physicals, Holsey told me that she was getting married. "You and Hildegard seem to have such a good relationship that I would like your advice about what it takes to have a good marriage," she inquired.

I used a sailing analogy in my answer, since she knew that we were avid sailors. I told her that a boat cannot have two captains at the same time, adding that just as we switch watches during a long voyage, so a couple must switch responsibilities as necessary. You guarantee foundering if both try to steer at once. I think a marriage will sink under those conditions. She nodded understanding.

When we moved from Berkley to Clinton Township, I felt that I didn't want to make the forty-minute drive to Holsey's office. Ruth Quincy, a sailing friend and nurse, steered me to Dr. Richard Stiphout, whose office at the Henry Ford Lakeside center was no more than fifteen minutes by car. "You'll like him. He's the best diagnostician around and he's a sailor."

As to the latter, we didn't have much time to talk sailing, because modern medical clinics all operate as profit centers on a twenty-minute schedule. As to the former, I really didn't have enough time to find out. Perhaps because of genes coming from some forebear, I'm healthy. Other than chronic bronchitis many years ago, which ceased when I quit smoking, almost all my encounters with the medical profession have stemmed from accidents or their long-term effects. It would probably have taken ten years before I came up with a medical problem for which I would need a diagnostician. But that didn't matter: Dr. Stiphout left after a couple of years to go sailing.

Before he left, he advised me to have a sigmoidoscopy because of my age and my family history of cancer. Tentatively arguing against it, I cited my negative hemoccult results over the years, along with my history of good bowel movements. Like the health nut in Bruce Jay Friedman's play *Steambath,* at 138 I had good bowel movements. I remembered the comments of my colleague Bob Donohue after his exam. He did not have good things to say about that long stainless steel tube. I mentioned Bob's severe discomfort to Stiphout.

"We use fiber optics now," he said, "we do it right here and it doesn't take very long at all." As a physicist with much experience in optics, I knew that the medics used fiber optics. I visualized a probe about an eighth to a quarter of an inch in diameter. I formed a clear picture of a new, but as yet unknown, adventure and agreed. The nurse made an appointment for the next week.

I showed up at the appointed time, after having applied the requisite purging preparations through both ends of the gastrointestinal tract. Quarter inch my eye! The device that lay alongside the examination table was at least as thick as my thumb and about as long as my arm. It did not look very flexible. Several tubes and wires connected it to mechanical and electrical devices on the floor.

After Stiphout explained the procedure and dangers, further stating that the nurse would be at hand at all times, I signed the papers indicating that I understood and lay down on my left side on the table. The doctor sat on a low stool to my back; the nurse faced the table at my front.

I don't know if the selection and positioning of the nurse was part of the procedure, but I want to give credit to the responsible person. Throughout the exam she stood quietly, latex-gloved hands at her side, her navel just about at my eye level. From the bottom of her rib cage to the mons veneris, this young woman had the flattest stomach I had ever seen. Her coral polo shirt and gray jersey slacks with 2% Lycra fit the situation, as well as her body, perfectly. Everything went in and on smoothly. After fifteen minutes of navel gazing, my exam was over. Stiphout said everything looked great. But then, I knew that.

"You may have some discomfort during the day because of the air injected into your colon. I've aspirated most of it, but you might feel some cramping. The discomfort will pass as the air leaves. It'll help if you move around."

I don't know if my buddy Phil ever had such an exam. I know that he would have enjoyed the after-effects of colonic air injection. Phil, in addition to some eminence as a physicist, was our lab's local fart expert. Some twit said that "Phil knew farts coming and going." I know he treasures the copy of Mark Twain's *1601* I gave him on one of our unbirthdays. I would have given him a copy of Benjamin Franklin's *Fart Proudly,* but I couldn't find it in our local bookstore, and I didn't want to steal it from the Macomb library.

In late afternoon, I could feel my rectum expanding as peristalsis pumped the air out of the colon. The fart that completely relieved my intestinal discomfort was, as we say in Welsh, *bendigedig,* spoken as you hold both clenched fists just above your head. I could not believe that such a thing was possible. Talk about Helmholtz resonators: it sounded a perfect B-flat, an octave below middle C.

Oh the time has come and now we must be parting.
And I know you really didn't like my farting.
So eat some scungili my darling.
Eat some scungili my love.

Twelve

"Birth of the Blues"

B. G. DeSylva, Lew Brown, and
Ray Henderson, 1941

Our local PBS radio station, WDET, carries a program called "Blues from the Lowlands" on Saturdays. I enjoy listening to it very much. It usually causes my wife to leave the room or, if we're in the car, to try to pay attention to something else. But it must sound better to her than another favorite of mine, "The Arkansas Traveler," a bluegrass program.

If it's just pickin', she'll get along without much sign that it bothers her. Just don't let them play something like Wilma Lee Cooper singing "You Tried to Ruin My Name," Laurie Lewis and Kathy Kallick chomping on "Is the Blue Moon Still Shining?" or even Alison Krauss's "Baby, Now That I've Found You." Her finger will mash some other station button fast as a frog's tongue on a fly. She doesn't understand that I like country music, especially bluegrass.

A bit ago, she said in response to my statement that I liked bluegrass, "How come I've been married to you for forty-six years and never knew that?" Of course, I had no answer. I do know she'd really misunderstand if I started playing the Clifton Chenier and Buckwheat Zydeco tapes while she's home. I suppose that I could say that it's all part of my studies in the propagation of Celtic music idioms through Europe and into America.

In part, the latter carries a lot of truth. In addition to simply listening to music, I study the sound patterns and let my gray matter look for relationships to other music.

Take Diamond's "Song Sung Blue," for example. Any reasonable person will easily come up with the *Elvira Madigan* theme as the source. When I hear either, in the back of my mind I not only hear the piano in the original Mozart concerto; my mind works on a correlation with the second movement of his clarinet concerto—the one that Pablo Casals wanted played at his funeral. To me, a strong correlation exists in their rhythmic patterns, and a weaker correlation in their melodic lines. I have a lot of fun with that.

I have a lot of fun with blues. If ever there was a severely constrained form, then blues are it. I mean, twelve bars, AAB, 145, what can you do with that? But listen! From Blind Lemon through Ray Charles and the new ones coming up, every writer and singer has something a bit different to say. To discover all the differences takes listening. If you just hear two hours of blues in the background, it might sound repetitious. You have to click your mental mouse and bring it up to the foreground.

You probably don't want to turn up the volume with other people around. It doesn't much matter what kind of music you're playing, if enough people are around, somebody won't like it. That's one of the banes of boating. You can be enjoying yourself at some marina, just looking at the water and sky, or talking with friends, when some power-boating dude decides to put his speakers in the rear cockpit and turn up his funk-a-delic CD to volume max.

Now I have no problem with any kind of music that anyone enjoys; I know that many people don't like to listen to what I play. But why do these turkeys think that everyone on the dock wants to listen to it? Even more amazing is that the dude isn't listening to it. He's shouting down the dock, between beer swigs, to his good buddy. Or he's walked away to visit some chicks.

It was a situation just like the latter that was cramping the enjoyment of a group of North Star Sail Club sailors on one of their annual cruises to Lakeview Marina in Windsor, Ontario. We had a most glorious day, what with a splendid sail, warm air, and sunshine enough with puffy clouds as we prepared for our hors d'oeuvres party on the dock. Then the dude cranked it up and walked down the dock.

A few of us gathered a bit away—Dick and Phyllis Parker, Norm and Norma Felske, Comm. Sullivan and I—as we commiserated on the problem with young people who have no manners. After giving each in the group a chance to speak, I went into my pontifical mode. I was well into my bull when a seagull decided to comment. As neatly as anything, he laid a glob of crap on my right shoulder with a wisp across my glasses. Because of the laughter, the eloquence of my delivery was forgotten.

I saw a bird drop a turd,
But no one said a word.
They all laughed when
He dropped it on me.

Thirteen

"Brush up your Shakespeare"

Cole Porter, Kiss Me Kate, *1932*

Leaving show business left me with no regrets. Of course, I was pretty young when that happened, so maybe that's a dumb statement to make. Yet, for about five intense years, show business was my life. It left a deep impression.

Every once in a while I see an advertisement for auditions at some community theater, and I get a twinge. There are several roles that I've often thought that I'd like to do. In general, I could probably do one from the panoply made famous by Stubby Kaye. In particular, I know quite a bit about "rockin' the boat," and I read *L'il Abner* a lot when I was a kid. And if it comes to ogling the Daisy Mae types, I could hold my own.

In contrast to Stubby's all-American roles, the role of the Wazir in Kismet has also caught my fancy. I feel the glee of sealing "him in a pot of glue"; the singing is in my range; you don't have to be tall. I first figured I could do the part when we saw *Kismet* in the round at the old Botsford Summer Theater out Redford way.

Even though the production didn't have Alfred Drake nor Doretta Morrow, it was excellent in every way. The fellow who sang the Wazir inspired me. I bought the original Broadway cast album of *Kismet* on vinyl just to hear and sing along with the Wazir. I got the malicious laugh down pat. The turntable broke down a long time ago so now I only sing the few lines I remember. Maybe I should break down and buy a CD version of the album. Then I could learn all his lines, in case I'm called.

Hildegard and I laid down a few bucks at the local horse track a couple of times; I used to wear a plaid suit; some of my friends think I'm a shady character; I can sing fugues. Those qualifications probably mean that I could do one of the tinhorn roles in *Guys and Dolls*. I should buy the CD version of the album so that I could be ready if I'm called.

What with my travels in London and Paris, my familiarity with Dover castle, which is pretty close to the sea, and being slightly cock-eyed, which is pretty close to being Cockney, I'm a shoo-in for a chorus role in *My Fair Lady*. I know the words to the verse of "Wouldn't It Be Loverly," so I don't have to buy the CD.

But the ro-el of them all, / That starts me all a-ravin' / Is the guy what sings the song / 'bout the bard of Stratford-on-Avon. I know all about kissing Kate: some people think I had a mistress of that name and still carry a memento on my car. Constant use has caused my copy of Willie's works to fall apart, so I know how goes *Troilus and Cressida*; sigmoidoscopy has shown that my *Coriolanus* is in great shape. When the call comes, I'll be right there.

In all seriousness, the wonderful poetry in songs by writers like Cole Porter impresses and interests me. I know an iamb when I see it, but I'm not sure about the trochee. I don't have the technical qualifications to expound about poetry in songs; my degree is in mathematics. But Philip Furia, as Professor of English at University of Minnesota has the authority.

His book, *Poets of Tin Pan Alley,* makes clear that it takes inestimable talent to see and apply the rhyming pattern that fits "British ambassador" to "Troilus and Cressida." What is more, the Porters, the Gershwins, the Fields, et al. continued the excellent writing in song after song after song. Today, when lyrics consist mainly of three to five words endlessly repeated, the average person probably doesn't appreciate the deep cultural background from which the famous composers of older popular songs drew.

Equally interesting to me is the kind of talent and depth that James Savage used in developing the theme, clues, and answers that he used in a crossword puzzle in the *New York Times Magazine,* 31 March 1996. The puzzle had the theme: Shakespeare comments about computers. Now how do you dig that out? One must have intimate familiarity with the ol' Bard to come up with the gems Savage used, although one might use a computer concordance to the same end. I prefer to think that Savage knows Shakespeare, and that his brain knows how to synthesize. These are the answers:

"The net has fallen upon me."	*Henry VIII,* I, 1
"There's magic in the web."	*Othello,* III, 1

"Mouse of virtue answer me." *Twelfth Night,* I, 5

"No man hath access by day."
Two Gentlemen of Verona, III, 1

"I put myself into thy file."
All's Well That Ends Well, III, 3

The determination of the questions is left as an exercise to the reader. No fair consulting Johnny Carson. The questions should be readily apparent to one versed in computer arts.

Fourteen

"Someone's rocking my dreamboat"

Emerson Scott, Leon Rene, and Otis Rene, 1941

To many people besides Scott, Rene, and Rene, a rocking boat means trouble, or discomfort at the very least. I'm blessed to have an avid sailor for my wife. We know many families in which wives are fair-weather sailors, if they sail at all. While the male member really wants to sail with his spouse, the idea, or feeling, of the boat heeling stops many wives from enjoying sailing. We won't even talk about the effect of real rocking.

Both Hildegard and I wonder why so many women have this aversion to heeling. We've taken many friends and acquaintances sailing. Never have we attempted to scare them. Indeed, we've gone out of our way, by reefing sails and selecting points of sail, to make the ventures comfortable and enjoyable. If the weather had gotten bad enough to frustrate our aims, we've doused sail and started the engine.

Although we've never had a single guest complain, on several occasions, the female commented that the boat felt tippy at times. Never has a male remarked so. That seems a most peculiar division of feelings.

I had wondered if some physiological basis existed to explain it. Do women, for example, have a different inner ear construction that makes even small deviations from the vertical distressing? If so, then not all women have it. Sailing annals are filled with exploits of sailing women from those who sailed to faraway lands in Phoenician times, through Ann Davison's single-handed crossing of the Atlantic, to Dawn Riley and the other women of the America's Cup venture. My teaching colleague Paola Nisonger sailed on Brown University's team as a student, and we talked many times about the joys of racing. Paola the mother became a *mutha* when she talked sailing and the pure joy of luffing up a competitor.

Have we instilled some false sense of delicacy in some women? What else can explain the anticipation of discomfort as exemplified by a passenger on our cruise ship. I was standing at the rail of the promenade deck of the 30,000-ton *Star Princess* shortly after boarding at Seward. We were still tied to the dock. Behind me I heard a woman say, "Oh! I can feel it tipping. I hope I don't get seasick." She moved up beside me to hold the rail.

I expected to see a wee, gray-haired, cane-bearing lady wearing a lavender print dress with a crocheted collar, perhaps with a shoulder shawl. But this smartly dressed lady probably was, at most, in her late forties, pretty good looking, as a matter of fact.

She listened to my reassurances that the ship used horizontal stabilizers to minimize roll, that the words Inside Passage meant precisely that (for the most part), and that the weather forecasters said we would have a glorious week. With her good breeding, she smiled and listened to me politely. The tightness in her face and her grip on the rail told me she would rather be on the dock: she could feel the ship rocking.

So how did Davison, Riley, Nisonger, Joseph, and other sailing women overcome that feeling? One possibility is that they never had husbands who were more than happy to reinforce an initial queasiness. A dockmate of ours went out of his way to keep his wife off the boat. He proudly stated that he told her that if she didn't like the boat, he was going to sell it and buy one she really wouldn't like. He did. Several times we saw him going or returning from a trip with a couple of young, bikini-clad babes beside him at the wheel.

Many men delight in upsetting women, and take every opportunity to let women know that only real men sail. Dawn Riley's a member of our local North Star Sail Club, as well as the Grosse Pointe Yacht Club. When she made the lecture circuit after her captaincy of the Whitbread around-the-world racer *Maiden,* she spoke here. I sat next to one of our members who grumped throughout her talk.

When Dawn asked for questions, he smugly asked her to tell about the most enjoyable part of the race. From his previous comments I knew that he expected her to talk about warm, sunny days sailing on calm seas up the coast of Brazil, clad only in bi-, mono-, or no-kinis.

Dawn answered that she really enjoyed surfing through the southern Indian Ocean in 50-knot air, 40-foot waves, temperatures near freezing, and icebergs abounding. Her eyes sparkled as she told of the joys of sailing at peak speeds over 25 knots and an average speed for several days over 20 knots. Touché!

Real sailors, male or female, know that rocking sometimes (apologies to Rolaids) spells relief. If you mention sea legs to a sailor, it'll immediately conjure the image and feeling of the physical adaptation to the rolling deck, and the stability that one acquires by subtle shifts in weight and body position during those motions. To a non-sailor, the words likely mean the rolling gait as sailors walk down the street.

A physiological phenomenon relates the two concepts. The orientation of the three semicircular canals in the ear's labyrinth permits them to function rather as three mutually perpendicular gyroscopes to maintain the body in positional equilibrium in our three-dimensional world. During long passages, as part of the sailor's adaptation process, changes take place in the body's interpretation of the constant orientational disturbances to the inner ear. In effect, the body tells itself that it's standing still, and not to listen to the ear signals unless they get very strong.

Put the sailor on solid land and watch them tip as the ear tries to figure out what's happening. Hildegard and I have felt the earth move many times when we stepped off the boat. Once, we had crossed Lake Huron from the Fishing Islands in Ontario to Alpena, Michigan. The smooth, ninety-mile crossing took about twenty hours. We arrived in Alpena just in time to take part in the festivities of the Sarnia to Alpena race finish.

Seeing the beer tent in the field, we walked toward it to get some eats and drinks. With dogs and suds in our hands we started walking around looking for familiar faces. We felt the staggers building up.

"I don't think I can walk," said Hildegard. We linked arms and headed for the nearest tree, where we slowly slid to the ground and relative equilibrium. But the slightest motion of the head caused the world to spin. "We gotta get back to the boat."

The boat seemed a long way away, but we made it. In about five seconds we felt at ease. In the protected harbor the boat hardly moved, but it sufficed to completely dampen our discomfort. Even Rolaids ain't that fast.

Go ahead and laugh! Non-sailors don't believe us. When I went through a period of motion-induced disequilibrium that caused me to bang into the wall as I walked from bed to bath, or lean to the right as I tipped my head down to read, Dr. Holsey kept talking about my dizziness. My explanation that it wasn't light-headedness, giddiness, or anything like that passed over her head. I was perfectly stable as long as I didn't move. I tried to tell her that it was exactly the same as the sea-leg phenomenon. The Antivert pills she prescribed made me sleepy but didn't fix the wall banging.

I thought that my sailing internist, Dr. Stiphout, would understand and be able to prescribe a fix. He left for his sailing venture before we got into it. I just don't let it bother me any more. If it gets really bad, I just have to sit on my rocking dreamboat. It spells instant relief.

Fifteen

"Do it the hard way"

Richard Rodgers and Lorenz Hart, 1940

I used to get very high marks on my yearly appraisals at General Motors on the topic of planning. Bill Freas was very impressed that I could write down a critical-path timeline for a project on very short notice. I did that because I never wanted to do any extra work. Not many people are as lazy as I am. I don't like to work at all, let alone do more work than is necessary.

That doesn't mean I don't work. I didn't accomplish thirty-six years of raises and advancements at GM, get patents and awards because I sat on my ass. Even after I retired, when we were rebuilding *ASTIGAFA,* I did work that Hildegard still talks about. The installation of the hardware to support an inner forestay required that I climb through a seven-by-fourteen-inch door into the anchor locker where I lay on my side with my leg still outside. Hildegard passed the epoxy-saturated fiberglass and plywood pieces to me on a cardboard slab. After about two hours I came out for a rest and then did the same thing on the other side of the locker. That was just one reinforcing portion of the job. It took four trips to each side to finish the strengthening. The actual hardware installation required working with stainless-steel straps, nuts, and bolts and substantial drilling in the same confining and physically pain-inducing spaces.

In order to install a new packing gland for the prop shaft, we had to rig a harness and tackle from the boom so that I could hang upside down through the cockpit access hole to the engine. Once in a while I could relax. Hildegard would lower me enough so that I could stand on my head on a boat cushion in the bilge. When my neck got sore, I'd tell her to take a strain to hoist me up a bit.

Removing and replacing the engine oil pan to fix a leak required me to lie on my back on the cabin sole with the upper half of my body cantilevered into the bilge under the engine. You want to work out the abs? Try holding that position as you reach upward to remove and later replace sixteen oil pan bolts. Our almost-sixteen-year-old grandson could probably do it with ease. But at the time I was sixty. As they say, "A man's gotta do what a man's gotta do." He just don't gotta do what he don't hafta do.

The nuns at Nativity and St. Anthony taught the concept of Original Sin as: "By the sweat of thy brow thou shalt earn thy bread, and in pain thou shalt bear thy children." I found that hard to believe. What kind of a concept is that? It's inconceivable that an all-loving God would resort to such terms. They sound more as if they came from Pharaoh's overseer speaking to Moses and the slaves. And, in spite of the fact that those words form the basis for the Christian work ethic, I think that many women don't agree with that curse.

On the other hand, I could be wrong. According to an article I read a long time ago in the *Smithsonian* magazine, women don't know how to work efficiently. As I remember it, the National Bureau of Standards put various sensors all through a house so that they could tell exactly how people moved through it and how they operated the appliances. NBS found that women work way too hard in housework. It seems that the women tested simply didn't know how to organize things. For example, after supper they would carry a few items at a time to the refrigerator, opening the door each time to put the items away, and returning to the table for another task. In dishwashing, they tended to put one dish away at a time after drying.

I don't remember if NBS checked on how men work, but I suspect that most men do no better. During my GM career, I had about fifty different men work for me. It always struck me as peculiar that they worked so hard to accomplish so little. What's more, they'd sometimes get really pissed if you suggested an easier way to do it.

Perhaps it is the antiquated economic concept of a fixed amount of work that governs worker's actions. Some must think that if they finish the job, there will be no more work and then they'll get canned. And some may simply not know any other way to do things. One of our departments had a young man who ran the stock room and seemed to be a blazing star. You never walked into the room but he was working. If he wasn't in the room, you could be sure that he was steaming down the hall, driving over to another building, or climbing up in the mezzanine to find some part. He also frequently told people about how hard the job was, but that he expended all the energy he did because he believed that it should be done right.

During one of his vacations, a young woman replaced him. She was a student in a GM Quality Management course I taught. In answer to a question I posed about how well managers knew the job that underlings did, she said that she found that it only took her about two hours per day to do the replacee's work. The supervisor didn't believe her. He told her that it was obvious that she wasn't doing the job properly. I believed her. I hope she bears her children joyfully.

Some people can't even make children joyfully.

An appliance salesman comes up to a farm and tries to sell a washing machine to the farmer.

"Don't need one, got a good tub and washboard."

"But it would be a lot easier for your wife."

"We like doing things the hard way."

Noting the axe in the chopping block next to a large pile of kindling, the salesman suggests a gas stove.

"Don't need one, got a good wood stove."

"But it would be a lot easier for your wife."

"We like doing things the hard way."

After an exasperating series of useless attempts to simplify the farmer's life, the salesman noticed a little boy running after the chickens. "Your son?"

"Yep!"

"I suppose you got him the hard way too?"

"Yep! Standing up in a canoe."

Sixteen

"Blue Moon"

Richard Rodgers and Lorenz Hart, 1934

When I was a lad, the Catholic Church used to have The Index. The Index contained a list of books we weren't allowed to read and movies we weren't allowed to see. I wasn't much into reading theology or philosophy, so the forbidden books did not much concern me. But, along with everybody in the Depression and WW II years, I went to movies.

I remember walking home from Nativity grade school down McClellan with Tony Salvaggio and Angelo Tunesi talking about what we heard about Hedy Lamarr in the film *Ecstasy*. As nearly as we could make out from our eavesdropping, Hedy had a fantastic set of tits that flopped around all through the movie. There was also something about seeing hair in one scene in which she walks out of a lake, and we weren't talking about armpits. We concluded that it was the T&A that put the movie on the forbidden list.

Newspapers in those days didn't have pictures that showed much skin, so the ads for even the most "vile" movies didn't show much. But an ad for *The Lash of the*

Penitents provoked much discussion—and lies. It couldn't have been more than a couple of column inches, because all art theater ads were pretty small. Ghosted under the text was a vague picture of a girl on a cross, confronted by a hooded figure bearing a whip. With a good imagination, and an utter disregard for the possibility that the lines at her neck, waist, and shoulders represented clothing, you could see that the girl's torso was bare.

With the tiny ad as our only real data, much of the discussion revolved about what one would do with a whip and a naked girl. Except for playing doctor with the Gucciardi girls, or with Tony and his cousins, I didn't know much about girls, but I did know about whips. About a year before, I had taken my savings to buy a small bullwhip at the Sears farm store at Gratiot and Van Dyke. Along with the genuine Kinfolk sheath knife obtained with Popsicle wrappers, high-top boots with a little side knife-pocket that my mother finally got me, and a red-and-black-checked mackinaw, I figured that I was a real outdoorsman. Because I didn't hit myself in the head or butt when wielding the whip, and I could occasionally get it to crack, the guys considered me an expert.

Angelo said that a friend of his older brother had seen the movie and the guy said that, in one scene, the whip hit the girl on the tit. As we oohed, aahed, and wondered what it was like on either the sending or receiving end, eyes turned to me, the fount of whip wisdom.

"Well," I started, remembering what I could of the Wild West shows my dad had taken me to, "I've seen a whipper take just the end off a cigarette from a guy about twenty-five feet away. So I guess with a small whip like mine you could probably snap her right on the nipple."

"Holy shit," someone said. "That might snap it right off."

"I'm sure it would, if you got it to crack at just the right spot," I answered the implied question, with approval from nodding heads. "You know. It's like we do at the pool when we snap a towel on a guy's ass. If it doesn't crack, then it's nothing."

Someone suggested that snapping off a nipple wasn't a good thing to do to a girl. With all our experience with snapping towels at the Foch school and the St. Clair Rec Center pools, the nodding heads became sagely nodding heads. Each of us had had to bear painful welts because of a buddy's accuracy. We all assured each other that we would be most gallant to women. I vowed that my whip would never touch a human. We sort of knew the Church was probably right in not wanting us to see bad movies like *The Lash.*

But how about *The Moon Is Blue*? I may have been either too young or too dumb, but I didn't know exactly why the Church had put it on the forbidden list. I was old enough by then not to be shooed out of the room when my mother talked about it with the neighbors, but I really never knew what was so bad. It's not that I had analyzed it and concluded that the facts didn't support the Church's position, I mean that I couldn't understand what they were talking about. I felt rather like the Sumatran native trying to understand how the Dutch anthropologist could walk on water in Holland.

Hildegard and I saw the picture while we were courting. I've watched it on TV a couple of times as well. I still don't know why *The Moon Is Blue* was on the list.

I may not understand the Church or the movie, but I do understand language well enough to appreciate wordplay. I remember a story in which a Broderick Crawford character sends his Judy Holliday girl friend to a very expensive and respected finishing school to bring her to a high polish. After a year away in France, the girl returns and the guy meets her at the airport where she greets him:

"Oh honey, I've been away for a year. Did you get blue while I was gone?"

"Can ya beat dat! I spend a fortune to send her to da best finishing school in the woild and dey don't even loin her how to use da past participle."

My wife read the draft of this section and we're discussing her suggestions. Now we're talking 1997, maybe forty to fifty years after *The Moon Is Blue.* I suddenly realized that the movie with Broderick Crawford, Judy Holliday, and William Holden that I had watched with my wife was *Born Yesterday,* not *The Moon is Blue*. Talk about misapprehension, misconstruction, and just plain mistakes. How could I so clearly remember my mother talking about it when she died in 1951, two years before the movie came out? Now I'm not sure that I ever saw *The Moon Is Blue*. About 1980 I did finally see *Ecstasy*. I don't remember anything really sexy, although Hedy was supposed to have an erotic love scene. The only part with tits that I remember was a fuzzy, distant shot of Hedy Lamarr getting out of a pond. Big deal!

Maybe that picture wasn't a big deal, but Ms. Lamarr was pretty big overall. In addition to her distinguished career in movies, she and George Antheil invented spread-spectrum radio during World War II while sitting at a barroom table. On August 11, 1942, the U.S. Patent Office issued her Patent No. 2,292,367. We would not have cellular phones without spread-spectrum radio.

Certainly, over the course of many years after her invention, and with the pressure of wartime needs, somebody else would have figured out how to do it. In the long run, we would have everything that we have today even without her contribution. But it might have come later. As one who has been in a technical branch of radio for many years, I will give great credit to Hedy for having done it first. *That's* a big deal!

Seventeen

"I'm always true to you darling, in my fashion"

Cole Porter, Kiss Me Kate, *1948*

Hildegard's father, Paul Dunnbier, had a charming manner and could carry off elegance with the style of one of the lower European nobility. I had never talked much to him about his education, but he had said that his Silesian "grandparents on both sides were, so to speak, serfs just like the Negroes here." He went to trade school in Germany to become a toolmaker.

Although his German accent was quite thick, his command of English was excellent. When he came to the States, he learned English by going to the silent movies with a friend who read him the subtitles. Although I don't know this for sure, from the size and scope of his library, I believe the command came from his extensive reading. He must also have read extensively while still in Germany. He could quote Schiller and Goethe easily and at length. No doubt his German determination helped him to accomplish much. Paul's father sent his sons to trade school so that they wouldn't be serfs. Paul himself determined that he would be a gentleman.

I didn't get to know him until some time after Hildegard and I married, but I thought he did fairly well on his goal. About the only problem I had with him as my father-in-law was that my own style was an economic notch or two below his. He frequently asked me how much I was making. No matter what I said, he'd say that as a tool-and-die maker he was making three times as much. The money helped him live in his desired style; that was my impression.

Hildegard and her brother Fritz had other impressions of him. Hildegard admitted that Paul could be utterly charming, but she went further than that. He was an audacious flirt, she said. I never heard much as to how their mother took all this. I did hear that at the many parties and dances he attended, he was sure to catch the eye of one of the ladies.

Fritz must have thought that some of this was pretty funny. When the Cole Porter song came out, he gave his father the record as a birthday present. Paul didn't think it was funny at all. I don't know if it was a problem of coming too close to home or what, but Paul got mad, busted the record, and fumed and carried on.

An old saying is: If the shoe fits, wear it. I don't know if there's a saying about what to do if the shoe pinches a little bit.

Nor do I know much about my own dad's relation to other women. If he and mom went to parties, it was at the American Legion Hall up on Caniff, where they mostly drank a lot of beer and spoke Polish. I'm pretty sure my dad didn't dance well, if at all. I had heard him say on several occasions, "My eyes never got married," sometimes directed to my mother, but more frequently to other males about. You probably can't go too wrong with that.

Ven I'm goink to the shvitz,
And I see those lovely tits,
With those shvitzy tits I vant to say "Oi vey!"
But I'm always true to you dahlink in my passion,
I'm always true to you dahlink in mine vay.

Eighteen

"Oh! Ma-Ma! (The Butcher Boy)"

Lew Brown and Rudy Vallee, 1938

"Chedda luna, mezza mani"

Traditional Italian

Italians made up the majority of residents of the *Cacalupa,* the region of eastside Detroit around the old DSR horse barns and end of the line at Harper and Gratiot. The horses were long gone by the time of my birth, and the streetcar line went clear out to Eight Mile Road, but the regional name stuck, and even non-Italians used the name to tell people what part of Detroit they lived in.

Like the Polish area around Joseph Campau and Chene, like the German area out Gratiot near Six Mile Road, and like the Hungarian area downriver called Delray, the *Cacalupa* had redolent air. In the days of horse-drawn streetcars, it was probably more than redolent. With the electric streetcars of my youth, the air carried cooking odors, although the springtime blooms of the catalpa trees, or the fall piles of burning leaves, sometimes overpowered the tomato, basil, garlic, and oregano scents.

Even though names like Salvaggio, Paonessa, Tunesi, and Gucciardi predominated in the area, the 5000 block of Crane Street had a strongly cosmopolitan flavor. The Meyers next door were Jewish; Mr. Paul, for whom my Dad distilled cherry wine into something more potent, was Dutch, along with the Rybecki family on our side; the black Terrell family, whose father drove a limousine for the Diggs funeral home, lived there for a long time; another black family lived in the southeast corner house; a Lebanese family, whose eldest son attended Nativity grade school with the rest of us, lived just north of the middle of the block; a couple of—I guess from their names—English families kept nice houses; and finally, the three Polish families of Joseph (nee Jozefiak), Blaskiewicz (related through a paternal aunt), and an obscure cousin called Crane Street home. The smells of scampi, rouladen, golubki, sauerkraut, kielbasa, smaltz chicken, and many varieties of breads and sweets worked like the trees and leaves to lend something other than an pure Italian flavor to the air at various times.

Like a man thrown overboard into icy, salty water who must learn to swim if he's not to drown, I learned to eat when immersed in this redolence. Today, when friends call about dinner arrangements to ask my wife what I like, she says, "Put it down in front of him and he'll eat it." That's been true for as far back as I can remember, save for creamed onions, which I couldn't keep down when I was at the American Legion's children's home. My mother was fond of telling how, as a four-year old, I came home crying that Mrs. Gucciardi, our next-door neighbor, wouldn't let me eat *bubbalusha* (snails) with them. Though I don't remember that incident, I remember many other *bubbalusha* meals at Mrs. Gucciardi's.

You bought *bubbalusha* by the bushel basket up at the Harper-McClellan market. In order to bring the critters out of hibernation, so that you could throw them live into the steaming sauce, you dumped them into a tub of water. In a couple of hours the snails would start moving about. Some folks used one of those zinc washtubs; Mrs. Gucciardi used the bathtub. To keep the snails from crawling away, you put a couple of boards and bricks over the top.

The perfection of the summer day that Mrs. Gucciardi chose for a *bubbalusha* dinner called for a trip with the kids to Pingree Park and its wading pool, or maybe to Belle Isle—if you had a car. The Gucciardi girls, Helen, Leah, Rita, and Angie, my sister and I helped dump the dormant snails into the tub and put the boards and cement blocks on top. That done, we all went to the park.

Like Johnny at the fair, we stayed too late at the park. When we returned home, Mrs. Gucciardi opened the bathroom door and yelled, "Mangia l'America!" The snails had revived, pushed aside the boards and blocks, and climbed all over the walls and ceilings. We kids thought that was great; we picked them off the walls; we wondered if free snails tasted better than captive snails. They did!

Mrs. Gucciardi used to say "Mangia l'America" a lot, particularly in times of stress. At least, I thought that's what she was saying. I knew that *mangia* meant eat, but I could never figure out why anybody would want to eat America. It wasn't until I reached adulthood and studied French in college that I realized that she was saying "Mangez la merde." It all went together, of course. Although I had always thought of Mrs. Gucciardi as Italian, she was really French-Canadian, having been born in Calendar, Ontario.

I knew quite a bit of Italian as a youth, but it all seems to have vanished. However, with knowledge of just a few words and memories of the sounds, I, along with Sid Caesar, can fake it pretty good. That worked to good advantage during a trip my wife and I took to France in early 1997. Our tour stopped for lunch at a crêperie. I got up to use the toilet, and, as I walked past the open cooking area, sang a few bars of "The Butcher Boy" in English. As I again walked past the cookery on my return to the table, the chef called out, "Chantez! Chantez, monsieur!" With open throat, open arms, a few words that I thought I remembered, and a lot of fakes, I complied:

> Chedda luna, mezza mani,
> Mama mia, mi madidadi.
> Zin zo, zin zo, zin zo, zin zo.
> Quella ve duce mesta viani
> Mostaciolli esquideba.

Ai, ai, ai, peschavici bacala!
Ai, ai, ai, peschavici bacala!
Ai, ai, ai, peschavici bacala!
Chedda luna, mezza mani,
Peschavici bacala.

It brought down the house.

Notes

Cacalupa literally means "where the wolf shits." When Italians populated the area in the mid- to late 1800s, the Harper-Gratiot intersection was literally at the end of the streetcar line. Only swamp and forest lay to the east. Although wolves were extremely rare in that part of Michigan by then, the Italians brought their description of wilderness with them. Today we would say "in the boonies."

Mangez la merde: French for "Eat shit."

Nineteen

"YMCA"

Jacques Morali, Henri Belolo, and
Victor Willis, 1978

I don't fancy nose studs. A young woman at the Mt. Clemens YMCA wears one. She's a college student named Beth and she works part-time there. I've observed her as she works out on the Cybex weight machines, the treadmill, and the rowing machine. I've overheard some women say that they're jealous of her; they say that her build moves many women to tears; their comments moved me to scrutinize her more closely.

Man! they were right. Cory Everson would be happy to have Beth as an example of what a body-shaping program can do for women. This sure isn't the YMCA that the Village People sang about.

In his book, *Bad Songs,* Dave Barry zapped that song saying that he didn't understand why people bend their bodies into strange shapes as they danced to a song about guys picking up guys. That's what it was like in the old days; but the modern Y has decreased the M emphasis in favor of F, which means either family or female. Our Macomb Y has just completed a competition with the Warren Y. Although the directors called it "Jingle Bell Jive," my observation is that "Jiggle Belle Jive" would have been a better name. Dave, you should know that in this modern era, Y's are full of great-looking chicks like Beth.

Although she works out frequently and vigorously, no sharply defined muscles mar her good looks with harshness. Her softly sculpted limbs and torso could inspire most any sculptor to chisel away at a marble hunk. Her face fits her body perfectly, and if it doesn't carry a Breck-girl kind of American beauty, it strongly resembles many faces in classic sculpture and painting.

I had watched her during our three-day-a-week workouts for several weeks without speaking to her. I was not actively pursuing communication, I simply mean that I had never even said "Good morning or good day," as I do to everybody whose path crosses mine. We were always at opposite ends of the room, or exercising too enthusiastically when closer.

Over time we exchanged hellos, she in a somewhat cool, perfunctory, Y-staffer manner. But one morning as I was working on the leg-curl machine that faces the aisle, I saw Beth striding purposefully toward the exit, workout bag over her shoulder, blond ponytail bouncing along with other body parts, and eyes fixed straight ahead. As I was thinking that there was no use saying hello, let alone a longer good morning, she turned toward me, flashed a pearly smile and said, "Hi! Having a good workout? See ya!"

We exchanged hellos, good mornings, and smiles after that, but we never talked until today. As I was filling out my workout form at the counter, she came in saying "Morning! You starting or finishing?" That led to a small exchange during which I closely examined her diamond nose stud. She rubbed her left shoulder and said that it hurt a bit.

"O, bechod! Mae'n rhaid i ti lacio," I said with genuine concern.

"What's that?"

"Oh, that's Welsh. It means too bad, you must relax."

"Welsh? Cool!"

I told her to take it easy on the arm work until it improved, and moved over to the treadmill to finish the morning's regimen. A minute or two later she started on the treadmill next to me. If we hadn't been on treadmills, she would have pulled far ahead of me as she easily steamed at four miles an hour to my struggling three and a bit. But as we maintained our mechanical adjacency we talked small talk.

I finished the walk and stepped off saying, "Ciao, bella," to her grin.

"How many languages do you speak," she asked?

"Barely one!" I finished my cool-down and stretch sequence, shook out, picked up my bag and headed to the exit and the hall where my wife waited. As I neared the door, another old couple with whom I usually exchange pleasantries came in. After the hellos, he volunteered that I looked pretty good for an old guy. I replied that it only looked that way on the outside: I'm pretty rotten on the inside.

Unknown to me, Beth was walking behind me and had overheard the conversation. As she passed and opened the door she said, “I find that hard to believe.”

“Oh yeah? You’ll find out,” was my witty rejoinder.

“Well I’ll be here Monday to check you out,” she tossed off with the door closing behind her.

I still don’t fancy nose studs, but hers doesn’t look too bad to me now.

Twenty

"Margaritaville"

Jimmy Buffett, 1977

We finished our excellent lobster dinner at Harris's. You can always count on a first-class meal at any of the three places at Little Harbor on Jost van Dyke, but we decided on Harris's when we saw them building the fire in the back for the lobster pot. A lobster cooked outdoors, eaten in a beach-front restaurant with sand on the floor, pretty much puts you in a Margaritaville mood when you're in the islands.

Because we heard the island band cranking up next door at Sidney's Peace and Love as we licked the last of the juice from our fingers, we figured a bit of boogying would be just what we needed to settle the dinner. With the band going full blast, Sidney's didn't do much of a dinner trade that evening: All the crowd were drinkers and dancers. As we walked over, it became increasingly obvious that we'd have a good time mixing with the denizens of a Jimmy Buffett dream. T-shirts, cutoffs, and sandals were the uniform of the night with the young boaters shaking their booties on the floor.

We pushed our way through the door, grabbed a waitress, and ordered drinks. We'd have to push a bit harder to get onto the dance floor, but that's what island nights are like. As our party moved away to survey the scene, I caught sight of a large bulletin board that appeared to be covered with business cards.

I moved close to the board to see who'd been here. Maybe I'd know some of the cruisers who make the BVIs their sailing ground. I didn't recognize any of names, but saw that cards from most of the countries in the western world were stuck up.

I stood and peered, my mind focused on reading; but a soft bump on my back shifted my attention. As I turned slightly to glimpse the beginning of an exquisite woman, the cultured, Eastern tone of her "Excuse me!" brought everything in me to present time. Those two words started a universe of thoughts pell-melling through my mind. She doesn't belong here, I thought. That voice is strictly Bryn Mawr. Wonder what she's about?

"That's okay," I mumbled as I turned to look at her. Ivy League went through my mind. Long blond hair that showed the results of careful cutting and brushing; a tan that only rich folks can afford; a short, crisp, white dress, made from that material I think they call piqué, with cutout sleeves and scoop neckline, and Italian shoes perfectly matched the mental image that I had been forming from her first word. I wondered what kind of boat she came on; I was pretty sure it wasn't on one of the grubby charters that the rest of us think of as real living.

Although I turned to look at the board, my mind was really on the conversation between her and her partner.

Her comments about the cards reinforced my idea that I was standing next to a Biddle, a Bouvier, or another of that class. Even though many of her comments were funny, they all were completely gracious. Her allusions to bays, boats, and boogie joints showed that she knew these islands intimately, maybe even better than Buffett did. Perhaps she regularly left Philadelphia to winter in one of those million-dollar houses that hang on the cliffs at the west end of Tortola. I was glad I had on shoes, white ducks, and navy turtle neck. I didn't feel completely outclassed.

I was about to walk away when I realized that I had a business card in my wallet. It was one of those "500 cards for $4.95" that you get from Walter Drake, Lillian Vernon, or any other junk catalog company. Even though I bought some as a joke, they did look kind of neat with an all-caps APPLIED GRAMMAR in dark brown on tan background with my name and address in smaller letters below. What the hell! It's a business card, and this board's for business cards. I found a bit of an opening near the middle of the board and pinned it up.

"Is that your card?" she asked over my shoulder, causing me to shiver with the delight of all that culture pouring over me.

With that opening, I had to turn full face to say, "Yes, it is."

"What the fuck kind of a business is that?"

The elation over her confirmation of the Ivy League background assuaged any shock I might have felt on hearing that word. Only a Bryn Mawr, Radcliffe, or

Smith girl would have had the grammar training to use words correctly in all circumstances.

A graduate of any other college would have ungrammatically said, "What kind of a fucking business is that?"

Twenty-One

"A dream is a wish your heart makes"

Mack David, Al Hoffman, and
Jerry Livingston, 1950

I frequently dream. My dreams mostly involve friends. Ordinariness marks most of the dreams: There are no monsters, nor Dr. Caligari-like passages, nor unexplainable changes of milieu. No! I just meander through fairly normal events, with fairly normal people, in fairly normal situations. Sometimes I can't explain why the car in which I'm tooling down Woodward has no wheels, but I just keep driving.

So when a dream is really peculiar, I remember many of the details, and can almost review it when I close my eyes. Last night's dream fell into that memorable category. If I were to tell it to a Freudian analyst, I sure the doctor could probe my unconscious to discover some dark secrets disturbing my psyche. But I prefer to analyze myself, and to take joy in telling it to you and thereby relive the time.

The cast: Stacey, a great guy who's the chief equipment maintainer at our local Y; Christine, a young art restorer whom I met at a Welsh class in Iowa; and me, just plain Bill. The setting: a summer evening in a small suburban house in a small suburban town.

I was staying overnight with unspecified friends. From somewhere in the house a male voice called out, “We’ll be going to the theater tonight, but there’s all kind of food in the fridge; just help yourself.”

“Okay,” I said as I moved with my plate of pasta toward the table and sat down. The table stood in a hall leading to the master bedroom. It became apparent the Stacey was my host. Every once in a while I’d see him move past the doorway as he got ready. The table was now smaller and closer to the door. I saw that Stacey was nude. I averted my eyes, but still occasionally saw him as he moved back and forth.

“I just have to touch up my hair and put my lipstick on,” came a female voice to my left.

I looked up to see Christine’s nude form starting to lean over the table. Apparently, the mirror hung on the wall to my right. Now I really stared at the pasta as I tried not to look. But it was impossible not to see some of her as she leaned farther over the table. In particular, I noticed her pubic region coming closer and closer to the upright fork in my left hand. “Don’t get your hair tangled in my fork,” I said as I woke up.

Twenty-Two

"My Back Pages"

Bob Dylan, 1964

I just happened upon the notice of the Cymdeithas Madog intensive one-week Welsh class on some Internet site; exactly where it was and why I looked at it are long forgotten. But something grabbed me, and pretty powerfully at that.

Christopher Brown, writing in the *San Francisco Chronicle* about Eddie Izzard , an English transvestite, said that Izzard's actions were "Not a Whim, an Urge." That exactly conveys my feeling at that moment about studying Welsh.

I followed the links to a phone number, logged off the Internet, and dialed Ruth Hall at the Iowa St. David's Society. She told me that the registration deadline was that very day, but that there was one opening left. She kindly accepted my assurance that the check would be in the mail, and told me that she'd mail all the official forms and instructions. Now I'd have to tell my wife about what an urge had gotten into me, and what the urge had gotten me into.

She understood. In fact, she seemed to know better than I why a retired Polish physicist would want to study Welsh. One month later she drove me to the airport where I boarded one of those commuter planes for the flight from Detroit to Des Moines, followed by a drive to Simpson College in Indianola.

Madog runs an intensive course. In one week they cram you with about the equivalent of a college semester. To moderate the intensity, they intersperse Welsh history, dancing, singing, and other cultural respites. Through all of this you are encouraged to speak and sing Welsh, even though you might be as rank a beginner as I.

It was my rankness that ultimately lead to my notoriety in the Madog circle. At coffee break on the morning of the third day I was washing my hands in the restroom when Basil Davies, the head teacher asked, "I say Bernard, do you work out?"

"No I don't, Basil. I'm about as lazy as they come."

"Well, you look pretty fit. How old are you?"

Having one day of Welsh numbers under my scalp, and wanting to demonstrate my ability, I said, "Saith naw," thinking that I had said sixty-nine, when in fact, I had said seventy-nine. I think that Basil's English reply was something like "Holy shit." I didn't think that my Welsh was that good nor that bad; his comment went right by me. Having dried my hands, I opened the door and walked back to my beginners' class.

Two days later it dawned on me that I had said the wrong numbers to Basil. Sitting in class with John, Gwyneth, and Gwen, three young classmates with whom I developed a close friendship over many pitchers of beer in the local bar, I revealed my problem. "I think I should tell him that I'm only sixty-nine. Whadda ya think?"

The unison reply was, "Forget it. He's probably forgotten, too. And even if he didn't, let him think he's seeing a miracle. You'll probably never see him again anyway." I agreed that it was probably forgotten, and promptly forgot it myself. We finished the week with the ceremonial Noson Lawen and Eisteddfod, and all went back home with good memories.

For a while, I didn't think that I would ever see Basil again. As the year progressed I worked on Welsh a bit most every day. When an e-mail message from Madog about the forthcoming 1998 course popped up one day, I told my wife that the next year's week would be in Berkeley, California, and since our daughter lived in Oakland, it might make sense to take a combined vacation-study trip for a couple of weeks. I sent in my deposit.

When the information packet arrived, I saw that Basil would again be the head teacher. Nothing peculiar registered on seeing his name. But on our first meeting in the hall at Berkeley, Basil remarked that I still seem to be as young and fit as ever. My conscience began to prick me as it had in Indianola. The week went quickly with the study load and the pub nights, and mental fatigue kept the conscience in abeyance.

We finished the last class on Friday morning. Student Leslie Dowdey, teacher Paul Birt, and I stood there chatting after the others left. "I have a little problem I'd like your advice on, Paul," I said, relating the *saith-naw* incident with Basil. "I really think that I should tell Basil the truth."

"I think that you have to do more than that."

"What do you mean?"

"Within minutes of your telling Basil that you were seventy-nine, he told several of the teachers. He said that here's a guy who's almost eighty, and he's singing, dancing, drinking beer, and kissing the girls. By the end of the day, most everybody was talking about you."

"That's right," said Leslie, "you were the wonder of the course. Didn't you know that?"

"God, no! What'll I do now?"

"I think that some kind of public statement is in order," said Paul. "Just say you didn't realize until now that you had made a mistake."

I agreed with them. During lunch I thought about how I could do it. At the after-lunch plenary session, Cefn Campbell, the administrator, gave me a couple of minutes to make a statement. With Paul's suggestion guiding me, I revealed all and apologized to Basil. I need not have worried at all. Basil thought that it was one of the funniest things that had happened in several courses, shook my hand and patted me on the back.

At the pub after the Saturday Nosen Lawen, Robert Lloyd Huber took a wonderful picture of Gwen Foulkes and me laughing. She had just said to me, "You sing awfully loud for a guy who's seventy."

"That's because last year I was eighty," I replied.

Ah! but I was so much older then,

I'm younger than that now.

Notes

Cymdeithas Madog: "Madog Society." Prince Madoc is the legendary Welsh discoverer of North America. The society's full English name is The North American Welsh Studies Institute. Check http://www.madog.org for more information.

Noson Lawen: "Merry Evening" A Welsh get-together with singing, skits, and droll stories.

Eisteddfod: Literally "Chairing," a Welsh festival, originally literary, at which the year's Bard is chaired, but now also a festival of other performing arts. The two Eisteddfods in Wales are of world renown, but local eisteddfod at all levels take place throughout Wales.

Twenty-Three

"Mr. Lucky"

Jay Livingston, Ray Evans, and
Henry Mancini, 1959

We boarded the *Regal Princess* in Acapulco for the trip through the Panama Canal and on to San Juan. I found out why they call it The Love Boat: I fell in love with a Welsh blackjack dealer.

On the next-to-last evening, as we steamed toward St. Thomas, a group of us waited for an elevator to take us up to the Deck 14 casino and dance lounge. Down the hall a bit, with back toward us, stood one of the casino workers, dressed in formal black trousers, white shirt, and vest. My wife, Hildegard, asked if I thought it was a boy or a girl. I told her that I had no doubt about the gender: that was a girl.

"How can you be so sure? That's a pretty short boy's haircut."

"That's one of the reasons why I'm sure. Only a woman or a fairy can have hair that great." I further explained that the willowy shape, from the neck down the back through hips and legs could not be that of a man.

The girl, just about my height, turned and walked toward us. Later, some of the women remarked about her striking beauty. My wife thought that she was quite cute. The boyish haircut perfectly complemented the model's structure of her face. She looked like the young Ingrid Bergman in *For Whom the Bell Tolls,* complete with the blond hair and slightly upturned nose.

The elevator doors opened and she picked up her pace to catch it as I held the door open. Just as she entered the elevator, I realized that I'd forgotten to take my niacin, and told Hildegard that I had to go back to our cabin. As I excused myself to make my way past the girl, she smiled, looked me in the eye, and said, "Thanks! I'll see you later."

It wasn't until the next day that I realized that she had assumed that I, with the others, was on my way up to the casino to gamble. I should have said that I was going up to dance, not gamble; but at the moment, fixed as I was by sparkling green eyes that matched her green paisley vest, an intense urge prompted me to blurt, "Your place or mine?"

"Why not come up to mine?"

"Fine! See you in about five minutes."

As my wife later told me, other folks on the elevator whispered comments like: "Did you hear what he said to her? He's old enough to be her grandfather. Of all the nerve! Etc., etc." Hey man, when you're invited to a *Twmpath,* you *dawnsio,* even if you're sixty-nine years old.

Five minutes later I was on the dance floor, where a low, plant-covered wall separated it from the gaming area. Until tonight, action had been kind of quiet in the casino. Even on the dance floor, there were usually only a few dancers. But tonight the casino had a fair crowd. Ding-a-lingings and coin-chinkings from the slots made their way over the dance music.

I could just see an empty blackjack table through the plants, and as I wondered where the dealer was, I saw her come in and open it. Before the crowd gathered, I could see her as she smoothly took the cards from the shoe and dealt them. In a short while she disappeared from view as an enthralled audience gathered around the players.

When the musicians ended their set and took a break, I walked about the casino, dropped some coins in the slots and rang up a nice cache. I wandered to the girl's table. I had played blackjack at our bowling league's parties, but this game was out of my class. It really moved. I didn't know much about this kind of blackjack, but I did know something about dancing. This girl's hands danced.

Much later, she took a break and came into the lounge for a Squirt. I walked over and talked to her. I learned that she was twenty-four and had worked for Princess as a dealer for two years, that her name was Glynis, and that her great-grandmother came from Wales to settle near Ithaca, where Glynis still lived. She had a vague memory of some St. David's Day celebrations when she was very young, and had occasionally thought about learning more about her family history, and maybe even some Welsh.

I told her about my experience learning basic Welsh in one week at Y Cwrs Cymraeg Calon America, and showed her how easy it was to say *shwmae, hwyl,* and *bore da* for starters. She appeared to show some interest, so I suggested that she look into it. I scribbled Wayne Harbert's name on a card and told her that he was at Cornell and could steer her when she got back to Ithaca. *Mewn cariad,* my heart pounded as I bid her *hwyl fawr* and went back to dance with my wife.

That night I dreamed about her. When I told Hildegard about it in the morning, she laughed and said that obviously the girl had deeply impressed me. The gist is that Glynis and I were electrical engineering students. We were in a class on advanced antenna design. Her brilliance at grasping the relation between Maxwell's equations and real antennas confounded most of the guys in class. She and I teamed up to design a cellular transmission antenna for our final project. Everything went smoothly until the very end. I wanted to use polished tubing for the elements; she wanted a suede finish.

I went into the problems of skin effect, pointing out that a smooth surface permitted electrons to flow more easily. She argued for suede, saying that it was not the electron, but the flowing electromagnetic field that was the determinant. She appealed to the idea of a dolphin's skin with micro-corrugations that let the water slip smoothly over the dolphin. I felt that her analogy had much merit, but still thought that the elements required smoothness.

She clinched her argument by telling me that she had on leopard-patterned underwear made from a new synthetic fiber. According to her, this material had a sueded finish, but felt as if it were perfectly smooth. "Here," she said, as she started to unbutton the top button of her blouse, "feel this and tell me whether it's smooth enough for you."

That's when I woke up.

The morning of our last day at sea, Hildegard and I, trying to get the last polish on our tans, sat in the sun on the pool deck as the ship made for St. Thomas. Glynis, in a modest orange bikini that contrasted sharply with the dealer uniform of last night, played in the pool with other young crew members. When she saw me, she waved, forming a silent *shwmae* on her lips. She jumped out and walked over to say that she had enjoyed watching us dance. I said I had enjoyed watching her deal. She thanked me for telling her about the Welsh classes, saying that she'd probably look into it, and bid me adieu, leaving the impression that we'd meet again.

Hildegard remarked that I impressed the girl as well, saying, "I thought it was just one of those shipboard shows, but maybe that astrologer who read your stars at the Tuesday party was right," she said. "You're entering a lucky period in your life."

"What do you mean?"

"Don't think I haven't noticed how many girls want to look at your necklace," she said, referring to the pre-Columbian amulet on a leather thong that my sister had sent from Colombia. "Don't you guys call those things chick magnets? Remember when we were in the BVIs in December? That native salesgirl almost dragged you across the counter to look at it. Then that redhead in the ship's jewelry store a couple of days ago, what did she say to you when you bought that gold necklace? How old is she? Is she Welsh too?"

"She said she'd have to come home with me to teach me how to work the clasp. She's twenty-four. She's Irish."

"See! That's what I mean about lucky. You made a few bucks at the slots. An Irish girl wants to be your housekeeper. And now this Welsh girl? You're getting luckier every day. But you don't know how lucky you are. Good thing I know that you're only a sheep in wolf's clothing. Otherwise I'd kill you."

I think she's onto something. At the Sunday pinochle games my uncles had when I was a lad, my Dad frequently said, "Lucky in love, lucky at cards." Maybe I'll take up blackjack.

Notes

shwmae, hwyl, and *bore da:* "hello," "cheerio," and "good morning" respectively.

mewn cariad: "in love."

Y Cwrs Cymraeg Calon America: "The Heart of America Welsh course"

Twenty-Four

"Hen Wlad Fy Nhadau" ("Land of My Fathers")

Welsh National Anthem

You can hardly go to any Welsh-based event without having to stand up at the end as they sing this anthem. In my limited experience of four years associating with people of Welsh heritage, I've seen that this song exerts a mystical force over them. Third-generation Welsh here in the States go dewy-eyed when they start singing. I sing along, but it's really not my land.

But I enjoy festivals, and the Welsh have them. A couple of weeks after New Year's Day 1999, I came across a Web site that told about the Hen Galen celebration on January 11 in the Gwaun Valley of Wales. The valley folk used the calendar from the days before Pope Gregory goofed it all up. I know that dates are pretty arbitrary, and that there really isn't much difference between the first and the eleventh of the month, but the very idea of going back to olden times has some soul in it. I planned to have my own Hen Galen celebration when we rolled the big 2000.

By the end of February I had forgotten my flash-in-the-brain. Spring, summer, and fall rolled around with nary a memory of my great idea. But when we started December with a very warm streak, and the meteorologists were predicting a warm January, the Hen Galen idea popped up again. All we need is for it to be dry with the temperature in the high fifties, and we could have a great outdoor celebration on the condominium commons.

I felt in my bones that we'd have the good weather, so I called some friends and a few sailing acquaintances who like good parties. I checked with my local beer store to see if I could get some Brain's, but it wasn't available. I figured that Newcastle Brown would do. With some Kowalski kielbasa and *kapusta,* a big mess of ribs on the grill, and *sgod a sglod,* if I could get Kelly to bring over his 20,000 BTU catfish fryer, we'd have a fine feast.

The weather turned out as I had wished; all the guests came. Tone-deaf Ed Francis, who swears he's Welsh, brought his big *Draig Goch* flag. Charles brought the old catfish fryer and took charge of the *sgod a sglod.* As midnight rolled in and I started to welcome Hen Galen, the ribs were smoking, and the party was cookin'. Gad! we were having a good time—until the township police came.

I had borrowed the 10-gauge salute cannon from our yacht club, along with a dozen rounds of ammo. I had been in charge of the midnight shoot when the modernists at the club had their party eleven days before. Even though the club's just a hop-skip-and-jump from the sheriff's river station, in years and years the deputies never said a word when we fired the midnight salute.

But I guess that the police in Clinton Township didn't realize that all the rounds were blanks. I had gotten off only ten of the dozen when sirens filled the air, and blue and red lights reflected off the buildings. I thought at first that one of my neighbors had gotten into the spirit, but, just as I felt something cold pressing against the base of my skull, I heard a voice say, "Away from the weapon, sir. Hands on your head, and up against the wall."

The tone of his voice told me he wasn't kidding, so I complied. He was pretty firm but not brutal as he pressed me face against the wall, told me not to move, and patted me down. When I put my hands behind my back as requested, he snapped the handcuffs on. Had I been a bit more sober, I could have pulled the old Houdini joint-expanding trick and then slipped away when the cop walked off to question my family. Of course, I realized that I didn't have any place to slip to, and the cop's partner had probably dealt with slippery characters before. She'd have nailed me before I got five feet without even letting her long, blond hair interfere.

Just about the time I began sinking into deep depression and remorse, as I thought I'd be taken in ignominy to the township's rundown jail, I heard the officer burst into laughter. He turned from the family, strode over to me (still up against the wall), took out his keys and removed the cuffs. "Your wife told me what's going on, sir, and showed me the Welsh flag. It's an old Welsh new year celebration?"

"It's called Hen Galen."

"That's not some kind of chicken joke, it is sir?"

"No, officer, it means the Old First Day using the old calendar."

"Well sir, one of your neighbors didn't know about it and called us. I never heard of it either, and I'm pretty Welsh a way back. Name's David Davis. Some great-grandparents came to mine coal in southern Ohio from a place called Bonnie's Pride in...ah...in ah—Hey, Marilyn, what's that song the Beach Boys sang I told you about? Oh yeah, Rhonda. And one of my grandfathers came to the UP to work in the copper mines."

"Yeah! That makes sense. A lot of Welsh came to the States to work in the coal mines, and some of them went with their Cornish friends to work the copper mines. Pontypridd's in Cwm Rhondda. I know the Cwm fairly well; been there just once, but spent a couple of weeks. Absolutely lovely place with old towns like Treherbert and Treorchy, Ton-y-pandy and Tynewydd, all of them poor, though, since Parliament stopped the mining."

"I've heard. Lotta my uncles and great-uncles were miners in that—what did you call it? A coom? Got quite a few cousins over there, but we don't write much."

"Oh yeah? I know a guy named Basil Davies over there; he teaches in Pontypridd; maybe he's one of them. We're going to be there in July and August. Maybe I could look them up and give 'em your regards."

"Wow! That'd be great. Wouldn't that be something if your friend was my cousin? I gotta tell my wife about this. I knew there used to be a lotta Welsh in Redford, or maybe it was Livonia. We didn't know there was any around here."

"Well you know, people move around. I even found a Joseph in the Welsh cemetery in California at the Black Diamond Mine park," I said as we shook hands. I thanked him and agreed not to shoot the cannon any more. As he and Marilyn walked off, I bade them a fond *pob hwyl.* I didn't tell him that I'm Polish.

Notes

Draig Goch: Red dragon, the Welsh national flag.

kapusta: Polish for sauerkraut. Kielbasa needs no explanation today.

pob hwyl: "All the best"

sgod a sglod: "fish and chips," colloquial Welsh for *pysgod a sglodion.*

Twenty-Five

"Brother, can you spare a dime?"

E. Y. Harburg and Jay Gorney, 1932

"When Bing (Crosby) recorded this song in October, 1932," says an Internet lyrics page, "one out of every four Americans who wanted work could not find work." There are few songs written by white guys with such poignancy that captured the "dark spirit" of the time as well. Although Charlie Palloy had recorded it a month before, it was Crosby's record that quickly reached No. 1 on the charts.

You don't hear the song very much these days. Oh, once in a while there's a TV special about the Depression, but the song's mostly forgotten. If you want to get a feel for what those days were like, you needn't spend hours reading or watching old movies. Just find a copy of the song and listen to it. Today, with RealAudio® and the Internet, it's just a couple of clicks away. With all our wealth, it's difficult to imagine that, within the lifetime of many of us, tens of millions of hard-working people were reduced to begging. Yet for most of the 1930s, this was a very poor country, but only in a financial sense.

The Depression and Prohibition overlapped from late 1929 to late 1933. These four years made for a combination that Charles Dickens might have written about. On the one hand, millions lived from hand to mouth; on the other, millions spent so much money on alcohol that the Mafia became rich and strong. I'm just old enough to have seen both sides during the last part of that overlap.

The rich side of my father's Jozefiak family made its money selling coal in early-1900s Detroit. My father and mother, although from the poor side and much lower on the income scale, had riches of mind, spirit, and character that left me with invaluable memories of growing up in the early 1930s.

I never thought that we were poor. I asked once why the Salvation Army didn't bring us Christmas baskets. Dad said that we didn't get anything because we weren't poor. As an adult, I finally figured out why we had money. My Dad had been a bootlegger.

Prohibition turned many ordinary citizens into lawbreakers. My father, Walter Joseph (he Americanized his name from Wladislaw Jozefiak in the 1920s), smuggled whiskey from Canada and sold basement-distilled hooch. His sister, my Aunt Lillian, made beer. Some of my early memories involve playing with bottle caps and the clinking of bottles.

As we were returning late one night on the ferry from Canada in our old sedan, my father told me to lie down on the back seat and pretend that I was sleeping. I didn't ask why, I just did what he told me to do. The bottles under the seat clinked on the rolling ferry and as we braked at the Customs station. The agent looked through the window, said something about the little boy sleeping, and waved us through. I didn't find out until adulthood that I had been a decoy many times.

The front-bedroom closet of our house contained boxes of small, flat bottles and corks. I spent hours playing with them and snacking on treats like potato chips and Crackerjacks that I found in a big, green, metal box that had a strap to go around your neck. Although I have no personal memories of this, relatives told stories of my dad filling the bottom of the box with bottles of hooch, covering them with a layer of snack packages, and then selling the stuff at Navin Field, where the Detroit Tigers played.

Many ordinary people drank beer, wine, whiskey, and hooch, even though it was illegal. But, as Richard Bak noted in his book *A Place for Summer,* baseball players in those days drank booze in prodigious quantities. Dad occasionally took me on visits to the locker room. It seems that he knew many of the players.

People of political, business, or sports fame frequented our home at 5319 Crane, near Harper and Gratiot, in the mostly Italian region known as *Cacalupa.* Whether the activity in those days stemmed from Dad's illegal business, from his early role in the automobile unions, or from his American Legion involvement, I do not know.

Although many people thought that Dad was rather taciturn and emotionally quiet, my memories are of a happy, gregarious man who took me to meet ballplayers and circus performers, to watch barnstorming aviators and wingwalkers, to see polo matches or to catch large sturgeon in the Detroit River. On one occasion, though, he was not so happy. I had told somebody about the basement still. His voice was dark and powerful when he said that I was *never* to tell anyone about the still.

As you might imagine, in those times of crowded cities you could hardly hide a still from the neighbors. It was legal to buy large quantities of grapes and squeeze the juice from them. Mr. Gucciardi did that and brought some of the results to our house for refinement. Juice in an altered state also came from the cherries picked from trees in Mr. Paul's and Mr. Rybecki's yard. Then there was the applejack that Dad frequently mentioned. After I published a short essay about Dad's hooch days, I received a call from a former neighbor who's about ten years older than I. She remembered Dad well, and told me that her fiancé worked for Dad in the delivery part of the business. Undoubtedly, many outside the neighborhood knew of Dad's prowess in this branch of chemical engineering. But I always kept my mouth shut after the warning.

Dad generally was rather quiet. But his buried volubility popped up at the many union discussions that took place in our home—the front room for the well-dressed group, the kitchen for the shirt-sleevers. Dad once introduced me to Walter and Victor Reuther in the front room. I later saw Victor several times in the kitchen. Though I really didn't know what it was all about, I knew that the union was important, and that we had a role in the Ford strike and the GM sit-down strike in Flint. When I was in a labor economics class in college as an adult, I met Victor and asked if he remembered Dad. "Oh yes," he replied, "your dad was little, but he was pretty tough and a real fighter." Dad had once sent me to get something from his dresser drawer. I had always puzzled about the brass knuckles I saw there, but Victor's remark explained it all.

The front closet with the bottles also had a helmet and gas mask bag from Dad's World War I service. While wearing the heavy helmet, I'd trace out the picture of a machine gun and the black letters on the bag. When I was old enough to read, I saw that he had written down all the campaigns in which he had taken part: Aisne-Marne, Oise-Aisne, Meuse-Argonne, Chateau Thierry, and others that I've forgotten. As a proud alumnus of the Red Arrow Division, he always wore its button in his lapel during his frequent visits to the American Legion Post on Caniff, where most of the veterans were also of Polish heritage.

I sat with him at the bar, drinking my red pop and eating Blind Robins, as he retold, with great animation, stories of battles in which the barrel of his Foch machine-gun got red-hot during heavy firing. Their company later received the American Browning guns, as the story went. I realized later that the drawing on the bag was of a water-cooled Browning.

My short career as a circus performer came about because of Dad's American Legion activities. As movies of the 1920s and 1930s attest, many small circuses traveled around the country. One was affiliated with the Legion. Dad started my training on a backyard trapeze long before I started school. My mother, an excellent seamstress, made a miniature acrobat costume for me that I wore in a few rehearsals under the canvas. I was supposed to ride a pony into the tent and would get to keep the pony as part of the pay package. But when my great circus début came up, I came down with the measles.

I really don't know how my Dad felt about the failure at the time. I do know that he was always proud of all my accomplishments as I was growing up. And I heard him delightedly repeat that pony and measles story many times. He usually ended the story by saying, "You know, he could have been a star."

Thanks Dad.

About the Author

Bernard W. Joseph, a native Detroiter and math alumnus of Wayne State University, retired in 1986 after thirty-six years as a physicist, optical engineer, and inventor. Since then, he's devoted himself to sailing with his wife and co-captain Hildegard. He's written boating articles for *Cruising World*, *Good Old Boat*, *lifeline*, *Sennit*, and *Northern Breezes*. He's now attacking other literary forms and has received several rejection slips. He received an award for a short story, but the calligrapher misspelled his name on the certificate.

He may be reached by email at k8lix@arrl.net.